Amazon Echo Show User Guide

Newbie to Expert in 1 Hour!

by Tom Edwards & Jenna Edwards

Other Books By Tom & Jenna Edwards

<u>Amazon Echo User Guide - Newbie to Expert in 1 Hour!</u>

<u>Amazon Echo Dot User Guide - Newbie to Expert in 1 Hour!</u>

<u>Amazon Echo Show User Guide - Newbie to Expert in 1 Hour!</u>

<u>Fire HD 7 User Guide - Newbie to Expert in 2 Hours!</u>

<u>Fire HD 8 & 10 User Guide - Newbie to Expert in 2 Hours!</u>

<u>Fire TV Stick User Guide - Newbie to Expert in 1 Hour!</u>

<u>Amazon Fire TV User Guide - Newbie to Expert in 1 Hour!</u>

Before We Start - Important!

Throughout this book we recommend certain webpages that might be useful to you as an Echo Show owner and user.

A lot of the webpages we recommend are on Amazon, and a typical Amazon web address might look something like this:

www.amazon.com/dp/B00DBYBNEE?_encoding=UTF8&camp=1789&creative=9325&linkCode=pf4&linkId=UPTTB3CK67NSPERY&primeCampaignId=prime_assoc_ft

The link above takes you to the Amazon Prime sign-up page, but that's a lot of characters for you to type! So we've used what they call a Link Prettifier to make the links shorter and easier to use.

In this example the shortened link is - **www.lyntons.com/USPrime** - if you type that into your browser, it will save you lots of typing time, but still take you straight to Amazon Prime....

Contents

Want the Latest Amazon Echo & Alexa News?

Before we start, we just want to remind you about the FREE updates for this book. The Amazon Echo family of devices are still in their infancy. The landscape is changing all the time with new services, apps and media suppliers appearing daily.

Staying on top of new developments is our job and if you sign up to our free newsletter we will keep you abreast of news, tips and tricks for all your streaming media equipment.

If you want to take advantage of this, all you need to do is sign up for the updates here: **www.lyntons.com/updates**.

Don't worry; we hate spam as much as you do so we will never share your details with anyone.

INTRODUCTION

Welcome

Welcome and thank you for buying the **Amazon Echo Show User Guide: Newbie to Expert in 1 Hour!**, a comprehensive introduction and companion guide to the exciting possibilities that this all-new Echo Bluetooth speaker and personal assistant has to offer.

Do You Need This Book?

We want to be clear from the very start - if you consider yourself tech savvy, e.g. the kind of electronics user that intuitively knows their way around any new device or is happy Googling for answers **then you probably don't need this book.**

We are comfortable admitting that you can probably find most of the information in this book somewhere on Amazon's help pages or on the Internet - if, that is, you are willing to spend the time to find it!

And that's the point... this Amazon Echo Show book is a time saving manual primarily written for those new to streaming media devices, Bluetooth devices and tech that works in tandem with your PC or mobile device.

If you were surprised or dismayed to find how little information comes in the box with your Echo Show and prefer to have to hand, like so many users, a comprehensive, straightforward, step by step Amazon Echo Show guide, to finding your way around your new device, **then this book is for you.**

Furthermore, as mentioned above, the Amazon Echo Show and other Echo/Alexa enabled devices are still fairly new in the big scheme of things and there will be new features, skills and services, not to mention Amazon Echo tips and tricks, appearing constantly over the coming months. We will be updating this Echo Show manual as these developments unfold, making it an invaluable resource for even the tech savvy.

Even if you are buying the first edition of this Echo Show instruction book, never fear, you too can keep up to speed with all the new Amazon Echo updates by signing up to our free email newsletter here - **www.lyntons.com/updates** - so you'll never miss a thing.

How To Use This Book

Feel free to dip in and out of different chapters, but we would suggest reading the whole book from start to finish to get a clear overview of all the information contained. We have purposely kept this book short, sweet and to the point so that you can consume it in an hour and get straight on with enjoying your Amazon Echo Show.

This Echo Show user manual aims to answer any questions you might have and offer Echo Show information including:

- What is the Amazon Echo Show and how does it work?
- What does the Echo Show do?
- How to setup your Echo Show
- How to setup Alexa
- How to manage your Amazon Echo Show account
- How the Echo Show and Alexa work together
- Amazon Echo Show tips
- Amazon Echo Show specifications
- Amazon Echo Show settings
- And a general Amazon Echo Show review

This Amazon Echo Show tutorial will also look closely at Echo Show features including:

- The Alexa voice remote (including Echo Show voice commands)
- The Amazon Echo Alexa app

- Amazon Echo extras
- The Echo Show shopping list and to do list
- Echo Show radio, music and news
- How to use Alexa Skills
- Echo Show smart devices (including home hubs and lights)
- Amazon Echo Show accessories
- Plus much, much more....

And for further customer support we have links to:

- Amazon Echo Show customer service
- Echo Show discussion forums
- Amazon Echo Show feedback
- Amazon Echo Show quick start guide
- Echo Show videos
- Amazon Echo Help Pages, help desk and community

As we will be updating this book on a regular basis we would love to get your feedback, so if there is a feature that you find confusing or something else that you feel we've missed then please let us know by emailing us at ReachMe@Lyntons.com. Thank you!

So without further ado let's begin...

1. WHAT IS AMAZON'S ECHO SHOW?

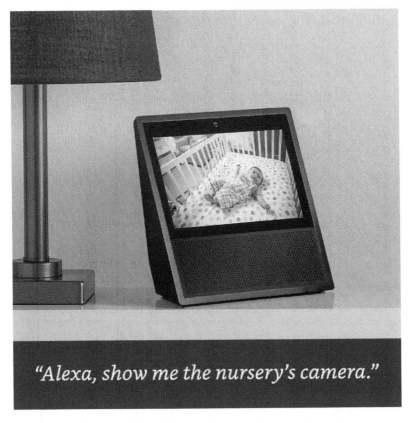

"Alexa, show me the nursery's camera."

Amazon calls Alexa a virtual assistant, and a very capable assistant it is. Alexa is accessed and put to work through Amazon's Echo devices including the Echo Show.

The Alexa/Echo Show combination plays many roles. It is:

- A versatile personal assistant we use to keep schedules, set timers and alarms, order food from local restaurants, create shopping lists at home to access on our phones at the store, and use for many similar tasks.

- A media player on which we listen to music, watch video and read or listen to books from a growing list of sources.

- A portal to shopping on Amazon.
- An integral part of smart home management from adjusting the heat setting to putting lights on timers.
- A wealth of knowledge, delivering a weather forecast, news, sports scores, information from Wikipedia and much more.
- An entertainment hub for games, trivia, jokes and more.
- A communication tool for talking with or without video to other Echo Show users among our family, friends and business contacts.

With its dynamic Skills section growing daily and third-party services like, the recently added, SiriusXM and Dish TV eager to partner with Amazon, Echo Show gets more useful all the time.

Does all its capability leave you asking: "Do I have to learn how to do all that"?

First, no, you don't. View the Echo Show as a tool useful for what you WANT to do. Just because Alexa and the Show CAN do something doesn't mean you MUST use it for that purpose. Sorry to shout, but we're eager for you to enjoy using the Echo Show without feeling any pressure. We've had the Show for six months and still haven't integrated it into our smart home setup beyond linking it with our Nest thermostat. We'll link it to our lighting, home security system and smoke detectors if/when it makes sense, not because we feel we must.

Secondly, there's no rush. Learn about the Show's capabilities and put them to use at your own pace.

Finally, this is exactly why we wrote this Echo Show users' guide - to make the learning process enjoyable, easy and painless.

Setting up Alexa and the Echo Show is very easy. From there, the combination makes technologically complex functions seem effortless, and it will take you just a few minutes, if that, to learn each task you want to try. Once you've had a few days to get familiar with the Echo Show, we're confident you'll agree. While we don't have plans to ditch our other Echo devices, we use them less often for tasks Echo Show can also do. The Show's hands-free usability makes it so easy. Just ask, and Echo Show delivers what you want.

Conversing with Alexa

If this is your first Echo device, talking to Alexa might take a few minutes to get used to. You're probably already familiar with talking to computers, whether it is Siri on your iPhone or the voice recognition systems that answer many business phones. It's no different.

The device's default wake word, as you know, is **Alexa**. It can be changed to **Echo, Amazon** or **Computer**. We like Echo and Alexa.

We've tried the others, but Amazon and Computer get used too much in our daily conversation, waking the Show to listen and usually respond with, "Sorry, I didn't get that" or "Hmm, I don't know about that." Occasionally it would start playing a song. All that was funny at first; then it became annoying, and we've stuck with Alexa.

Changing the wake word in **Settings** is simple, and we'll discuss it in the **Settings Chapter** - or you can go exploring for it yourself.

Speaking of wake words, we don't always use one in this guide when suggesting things to say to Alexa. Just remember that Alexa won't wake to listen to your request if you forget to use it.

How Does the Show Compare to the Rest of the Echo Family?

We wouldn't blame you if you felt a bit overwhelmed by the number of Echo devices recently released by Amazon. Things were pretty straight forward when you only had the Echo, Echo Dot and Echo Tap (the portable Echo) to choose from.

Now, as of October 2017, Amazon has added the New Echo, Echo Plus, Echo Show, Echo Spot and Echo Look into the mix, all at different price points and each with different features. The good news is that at least one of these Echo devices will be right for you and at the right price. The slightly less good news is that you will have to work out which one to choose!

We're assuming (always problematic!) you've bought this book to help you with your new Echo Show but let's take a moment now to look briefly at all options in case there's a further device that you think would work well in your household.

All-New Echo: The 2nd generation Echo is smaller and cheaper than its predecessor, we think it's more stylish too with its choice of finishes. If you've bought the Echo Show we're not sure why you would need an Echo, you'd probably be better off with an extra Echo Dot or Echo Spot.

Echo Plus: The all new Echo Plus is really more like the 1st generation Echo but with an integrated smart home hub. It's the same size as the original Echo, has an improved speaker system and, as mentioned, a built in smart home hub. The integrated hub makes connecting to smart home devices easier for sure, but it's not essential.

We already use a Wink hub to get our smart home devices online so adding the Echo Plus to our home doesn't really make any sense, we're already set up. If you're new to smart home devices and want to jump in, then the Echo Plus would be a great device to buy. If you feel lukewarm about the smart home revolution, then we would suggest sticking with the standard Echo for now.

Echo Dot: The Echo Dot is basically a mini Echo. It only has a tiny speaker so isn't the best way to listen to music but it can be plugged into any other sound system in your home and it has all the Alexa features and functionality. If you think of the Echo as the main device for your living room then the Dot is the perfect addition for a bedroom. At just $50 it's perfect if you want Alexa in every room of your house.

Echo Show and Echo Spot: These two new devices are basically the Echo and the Echo Dot but with screens! It's as simple as that. If you prefer to see rather than just hear the information and entertainment that Alexa provides then these two are for you. We have both and like both, but you need to decide if you need another screen in your life. The screens on both devices are small so it's not as if you'll be likely to watch a movie on them when you can watch on a TV or tablet.

The Echo Show is, we think, the top of the line Echo device so kudos to you for your new purchase. The Echo Spot is a very tempting addition to your Echo household as at $129.99 (at the time of writing) it doesn't feel like an extravagance. If you like the visual aspect of having an Echo with a screen then the Spot is your budget friendly option.

2. SETTING UP YOUR ECHO SHOW

OK, let's open the box and get started!

In the box should be:

- The Echo Show
- A 6' power cord
- Echo Show Things to Try card
- Tri-fold Startup Guide

The screen, speaker and power cord plug are covered with plastic for protection during shipping but should be removed now.

Where to Put Your Echo Show

We tried several locations including the kitchen counter and a dresser in the bedroom. The Echo Show gets moved once in a while, but we chose a small writing desk in the kitchen as its "normal" spot because it is centrally located to the kitchen and living room, the places we use the Show most.

Per Amazon's instructions, Echo Show should be 8 inches from windows and walls to reduce the chance of noise or echoes causing communication issues and false "wakes." The device should also be at least 10 feet away from microwave ovens and baby monitors to prevent their activity from disrupting Echo Show performance.

Now, let's Set up Your Show.

Step 1. Download the Alexa App to Your Phone and/or Tablet

When Echo Show turns on, it will search for the app to pair the devices. It will save delays and complications if you download it first.

Unless your phone or tablet is 5+ years old, you should be able to download the app to both. The device must meet one of these software requirement:

Mobile device requirements are:

- Android 5.0 or higher
- iOS 9.0 or higher
- FireOS 3.0 or higher

Check **Settings >About** on your phone to see its operating system version.

Now on your phone or tablet go to the app store for that device and search for *"Alexa app"*, and then follow the download prompts.

The app for PC or Mac is found online at **alexa.amazon.com**. Sign into your Amazon account there, and the app will be displayed.

There are three ways to interact with Echo Show, the touchscreen, voice requests and the app. A limited number of tasks can be done on the touchscreen. The app and voice are much more useful, and you can use either for a wide range of tasks such as adding items to a shopping list. Some tasks, such as changing the wake word, can only be done on the app. That's why it is important to download it in the early going. We'll explore it in detail soon.

Step 2. Turn On Echo Show

Once you've unpacked the Echo, plug the power cord into the receptacle on the back near the bottom. The On/Off button is the button on the left when looking at the screen. It's marked with a circle with a line through it.

When your Echo Show powers up, you might see **"Optimizing"** on the screen with a progress bar. The process takes less than five minutes to complete.

Step 3. Connect Echo Show to Your Wi-Fi Network Using Onscreen Prompts:

- Select your language
- Choose your Wi-Fi network
- Type in the network password (available on back of your router or from your internet provider)
- Enter your Amazon password, if asked
- Read Echo Show Terms and Conditions

In rare cases, a preferred network won't show up in the list. Tap **Add a Network** on the screen and:

- Type in its SSID using the digital keypad that appears or
- Tap the white microphone in the middle of the page, and when it turns blue, speak the SSID
- Select **Done** when finished

There are multiple ways to do most tasks like this on Echo Show. For example, you can also reconnect to Wi-Fi using the Echo Show Settings:

- Place two fingers or your thumb on the screen above the display, and slide down
- Tap **Settings** and then **Wi-Fi** (and if the device is connected, the name of the network will appear)
- View and select from available networks or choose **Add a Network** and proceed as outlined above

Note that Echo Show won't connect to ad-hoc or peer-to-peer networks because they are often unsecure.

Step 4. Watch the Echo Show Introduction Video

It's less than two minutes. Optionally, use the touchscreen to drag the progress bar to the end. After the video, and once you're connected to Wi-Fi, Alexa will let you know, "Your Echo Show is ready." That's a fun moment, knowing it's time to start exploring this impressive and useful device.

Step 5. Troubleshoot Echo Show Connection Issues

Most of you won't have issues. If you do, the light bar on Echo Show will be orange (more on the light bar shortly).

These tips resolve most issues:

- Turn on or reset your router by unplugging it and plugging it again after 15 seconds
- If your network appears in the list, but Echo Show won't connect, tap the network, and tap **Forget** to reset it before trying again to connect
- Double-check your Wi-Fi and Amazon passwords, and try again
- Free up bandwidth on the network by turning off other connected devices
- If your Wi-Fi network has a 5.0 GHz frequency in addition to the standard 2.4GHz connection, try both
- If Wi-Fi becomes intermittent, unplug the network hardware (router and modem, if not combined in one unit) and unplug Echo Show for 15 seconds or more before plugging and restarting them
- If the Echo Show doesn't connect to Wi-Fi, repeat Step 2

Step 6. Pair your Phone and Tablet with the Echo Show

This is an optional step for those that want to use Echo Show's Bluetooth capabilities to play music streamed from a music account on their phone or tablet. The first time you pair a mobile device we recommend you use the Alexa app via your PC or Mac and follow these steps:

- Make sure **Bluetooth** is turned on in the **Settings** section of your mobile phone or tablet
- Now go to into your Alexa app and visit **Settings >Your Echo Show > Bluetooth > Pair a New Device**
- When you click/tap **Pair a New Device** a page will open and search for "Available speakers" to connect to. **Tip:** You have

already turned on Bluetooth on your mobile, but also make sure that the phone/tablet is active, that's to say not in sleep mode.

- Your phone or tablet should now appear as an option so go ahead and click on it.

- Your mobile device will probably flash up a message asking you to confirm that you want to pair it with your Echo, so go ahead and confirm.

- A single chime will sound to indicate the device has been paired, and Alexa might say "Now connected to [your device]"

From now on you can unpair or pair this mobile device by simply saying "**Alexa disconnect**"or "**Alexa, connect**"

Repeat this process for every new device you want to pair with Alexa.

Also be aware that you can only pair one Bluetooth device at a time. If you've paired several devices to Echo Show, it will connect to the most recently paired device when you make the request.

To change from one mobile device to another you have to return to **Settings > Your Echo Show > Bluetooth** and manually disconnect from the current connected device before reconnecting to a different device.

When a Bluetooth device is paired to your Echo Show, you'll enjoy hands-free control with commands such as, "**Alexa...**

- *Play"*
- *Pause"*
- *Previous"*
- *Next"*
- *Stop"*
- *Resume"*
- *Restart"*

It should be stressed that before you can use these commands you need to start playing something via your paired device - play an album in your iTunes app for example.

We found through experience that, though the information is on Amazon too, if you try to request specific songs, albums or artists from the music stored on your phone or other Bluetooth device, the Echo Show will disconnect from the device and search for the music in your Amazon Music library.

So you can only use these voice commands to control content that is already playing.

3. THE ECHO SHOW'S PHYSICAL FEATURES AND ACCESSORIES

Now that your Show is connected and usable, let's explore its features and what they do.

There are three buttons on top surrounded by an elongated circle of tiny holes that let in sound for the 8 microphones that give the Show the ability to listen in all directions.

The button on the left has these functions:

- **Turn on Echo Show** by pushing it.

- **Turn off Echo Show** by holding it for several seconds, then touching **OK** on the screen.

- **Turn off the microphones and camera** when your Echo Show is on by pressing it and releasing it within a couple seconds. A small red light above the display will light and stay lit. A circle with a line through it will appear in the display, and the light bar will turn red. The circle and bar light will

15

darken after a few minutes. When the microphones are off, Alexa won't respond to the wake word. In this mode, an Alexa Voice Remote is needed to communicate with Alexa and Echo Show.

The button in the center turns your volume down. The button on the right turns your volume up.

Now, let's explore the front of the Echo Show.

- **Picture/video camera:** The 5mp camera takes crisp pictures and can be used for video chats. We'll discuss this in the section on Drop Ins (**Chapter 15**).

- **Touchscreen:** 7-inch diagonal, 1024 x 600 resolution that we think is quite good

- **Light Bar:** The bar is located across the bottom of the screen and lets you know what's happening with Echo Show.

  1. **No lights (but Echo Show is turned on):** Alexa is ready for action.

  2. **Blue at the edges, green toward the center:** Alexa is listening for your request.

3. **Blue:** Alexa is working to fulfill your request

4. **Orange:** Wi-Fi isn't working, a topic covered in the section on troubleshooting common problems (**Chapter 14**)

5. **Purple:** You've turned on "**Do Not Disturb**." It is accompanied by a crescent moon. You won't get notifications and nobody can drop in on you when Show is in this mode. **Notifications** and **Drop In** are explained below.

6. **Red:** The camera and microphones are tuned off.

Inside the Echo Show are dual 2-inch speakers.

If you like specs, here are the Show's:

- The front is 7.375 inches square
- The base is 3.625 inches deep at the bottom
- The Show weighs 2lbs, 9oz
- The screen is 7 inches diagonal
- Echo Show has an Intel Atom x5-Z8350 processor

Echo Show Accessories

Accessorizing Echo Show has aesthetic and functional value. Most accessories are manufactured by third-part companies rather than Amazon. They include:

- A variety of covers, some with handles for easy carrying
- Stands and wall-mounted shelves
- Screen protectors
- Camera covers for privacy
- Alexa Voice Remote stands

The Echo Show is backed by a one-year warranty. Third-party extended warranties of an extra 1-3 years are available.

The Alexa Voice Remote is optional and costs about $30. Its value is in allowing you to make requests from a distance when there is noise interference between you and the device or you don't want to speak loudly.

Requests you make are digitized and sent to the Echo Show. We have a remote, and it works fine, but after collecting dust for a few months, it was put in the gadget drawer and is rarely used.

There are two concerns many users have about the Alexa Voice Remote.

First, its voice recognition and communication capabilities are mediocre, so more commands/requests than usual will be confused. Secondly, in the past, they have simply stopped working at an unacceptably high rate. Amazon has stopped production of the remotes several times to work out the bugs, so read a handful of recent negative reviews to learn what the current issues are before you buy one.

One other consideration, as mentioned you can only pair one Bluetooth device to your Echo Show at a time, so if you buy and pair the remote you won't be able to pair your mobile phone and the Echo Show at the same time.

If you plan to purchase one, make sure it is the Alexa Voice Remote and not an Amazon Fire TV remote. **They are not interchangeable**.

If you have the Fire TV Stick with Alexa Voice Remote (currently about $40), that is a combination remote that will save you money over buying two remotes.

If you purchase one, you'll need to pair it with Alexa via the Echo Show:

- In **Settings**, scroll down (by swiping up) until **Device Options** appears, and tap it
- Scroll until **Pair Alexa Voice Remote** appears, and tap it
- Alexa will speak brief instructions and show them on the screen for you to follow

By the way, the best way to scroll through any page of the Settings is to rest your fingers on top of the Echo Show and use your thumb to scroll up and down. It allows you to control scroll speed and narrow in on what you want to select.

Personalizing Your Echo Show

The Show's default background image, sounds and what appears on the screen can be personalized in many ways. We'll show you how later when we discuss pertinent topics like the Echo Show Photos and Notifications. A few quick topics here will get the discussion rolling.

Echo Show Menu: When you swipe down from the top of the display portion of the screen, the Show's menu appears where you can:

- **Adjust Settings:** Feel free to explore **Settings** at your leisure. Settings are the subject of a lengthy later chapter in which we discuss settings on the Echo Show and the Alexa app on your smart device and/or computer.
- **Change the brightness:** Touch the dot at the end of the blue line that shows brightness level, and drag it right for brighter and left for dimmer.

- *Turn Do Not Disturb on or off:* Echo Show will remain quiet until you tap the screen or make a request.

Trending Topics: A handful of Trending Topics rotate constantly on the screen in default mode. Tap them, and the full story will be displayed. Amazon calls them "curated stories and videos." You might call them a nuisance. Or you might not. But if you do, you can turn them off:

- Slide down from above the display to show the menu
- Tap *Settings*, then *Home Screen* and then *Home Card Preferences*
- Scroll down the page by swiping up until you see *Trending Topics*
- Tap **Trending Topics** and then tap the oval *on/off* toggle (Blue means on; white means off)
- When you want to know what's trending, return here and toggle the switch back on

Darken the screen: Say, "*Alexa, turn off the screen*," and it will go dark until you tap the screen or make a request.

Ambient clock: Do you like having a clock on the screen when nothing is playing? To turn it on, go to *Echo Show Settings* and:

- Tap *Display*
- Tap the *Ambient Clock oval* to turn it on or off

Theme: Until you add your own photos, the default background picture will be provided by Alexa. You must choose one of three options:

- Photo (Default)
- Light background/dark text
- Dark background/light text

Go to *Settings* and tap *Display* and then *Theme*. Tap the option you want.

We use the dark background/light text option most of the time, especially when working near the Show. It is subdued and calming.

Trending Topics is always off. When we're not working near the device, we sometimes put on a Slideshow.

At the bottom of the screen, Alexa is always suggesting things to try. Currently, my screen shows: Try "***Alexa, show me popular movies***."

You can't remove this feature from the Home screen. Your only option in **Settings** and **Home Card Preferences** is to select **Rotate Once**, which keeps each option on your screen or **Rotate Continuously** for them to change every few minutes.

4. THE ALEXA APP

Our attention to this point has been on the Echo Show device. Now it's time to explore what Amazon calls the brain of all Echo devices, the Alexa app. In **Chapter 2** we covered downloading it to your smart devices and/or using it on your personal computer. So now's the time to download the app, if you haven't done it yet, or open up the app on your home computer (recommended) at **alexa.amazon.com**

The Menu currently includes these options, in order:

- **Home:** When Home is selected you will see some *Things to Try* and your list of cards.

- **Now Playing:** Shows you in detail exactly what you are currently listening to.

- **Music, Video & Books:** This is where you can find info on your Amazon Music Library, Prime Music subscription, Spotify, Pandora, iHeartRadio, TuneIn, Audible and more.

- **Lists:** Create shopping or To-do lists manually or by voice

- **Reminders & Alarms:** Here you can setup and manage multiple reminders, alarms and timers.

- **Routines:** A feature that allows you to activate several functions with one voice command.

- **Skills:** Discover all the third part apps that add further functions and features to your Echo Show

- **Smart Home:** This is where you connect your smart home devices to your Echo Show

- **Things to Try:** Not to be confused with the small selection of novelty items previously discussed on your Home page. This list is a great resource for keeping up to date with developments and trying out features.

- **Settings:** We'll refer to Settings throughout this guide to help you manage your Amazon Echo Show and account. And we have a chapter dedicated to this important section.

- **Help & Feedback:** Valuable guides can be found here to help you with every aspect of Alexa and your Echo Show

All Menu options and features are shown to the left when viewing the app on a computer. On a smart device, the menu appears as three horizontal lines. Tap them, and the *Menu* will appear with two slight differences, the Home page and the Now Playing page aren't listed.

For the *Home page* tap the small house icon bottom left of the screen and for the *Now Playing page* tap the icon that looks like three volume levels, bottom right.

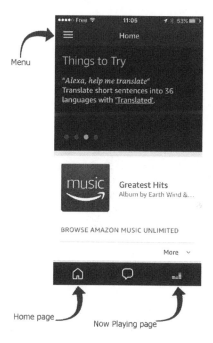

Our game plan is to take these Menu options in order, and give you a chapter on each. We've considered starting at Settings because so many functions involve Settings adjustments.

However, to maintain a systematic approach, we will keep the order and refer to Settings when needed. Then, we'll round out what hasn't been covered in **Chapter 16** (the Settings Chapter).

We believe it's the most helpful way to work through the information.

When a task can also be completed using the Echo Show screen, we'll point that out and explain how it's done.

Troubleshooting Tip: Do you have two Amazon accounts? If your Echo Show and Alexa app are not working together, it is possible that you did not register your Echo Show on the same account you're accessing the app with. One of these solutions will work:

- Access the app on the same account you used to register the Echo Show
- Deregister the Echo Show on the "wrong" account, and reregister it on the account you want to use it with

If you choose to deregister the Echo Show:

- Go to **www.amazon.com/mycd**
- Choose the tab called *Your Devices*
- Select the *Actions* box for the Echo Show
- In the popup window, choose *Deregister*
- Follow the onscreen prompts
- Return to **Chapter 2** and follow the instructions to register/ setup your Echo Show on the "right" account

5. THE ALEXA APP HOME PAGE

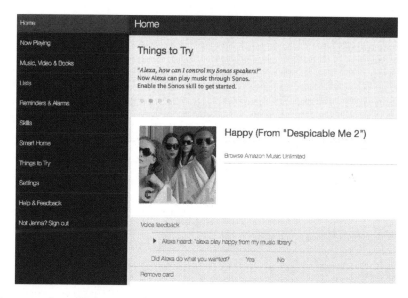

Three to five ***Things to Try*** topics rotate at the top of the page and change from week to week. You can watch them change or select the shaded buttons to move through them more quickly. And, of course, you can give them a try like, "***Alexa, Give me a limerick***," or "***Alexa Is United flight 7700 on time***," are two that are scrolling on my screen now.

Below Things to Try you will see your dialog cards. One card is created for each vocal request or command that you give to Alexa. So if you haven't yet asked Alexa for anything why not choose one of the Things to Try now. After you've finished you should see a card appear with information of the request you made.

To the right of each card you will see the word **More** and a down arrow, clicking or tapping here will give you the option to provide feedback to improve your Amazon Echo's voice recognition. What Alexa heard is listed with the question, "Did Echo hear you correctly?" Answer ***Yes*** or ***No***. You've also got the option to remove the card.

At first, we gave feedback and deleted a few cards to reduce clutter, but we mostly forgot about it pretty quickly.

Now the only time we choose the down arrow and give feedback is if the Echo did not hear us correctly, a rare occurrence. We also occasionally scroll back through the cards to locate a song/playlist/station we enjoyed but forgot to get the name of.

Depending on the type of request that produced the card, you'll have more options. For example, if you've requested Echo to play something from your Amazon Music Library, the card includes options to **Search the Amazon Digital Music Store** for similar music, **Search Amazon Prime** for free music and Browse your library for similar choices.

Cards for information requests will include the option to **Search Bing** for the topic.

If you choose the **Learn More** option in blue on any card or at the top of the list of cards, the Alexa FAQs appear.

You can manage the history of your dialog with Amazon Echo in much the same way as you manage your computer's history. Go to **Settings > History** where you'll find the complete list of requests and commands.

We occasionally scroll down the list to find a station we were playing or retrieve an answer to a question we asked. Provide feedback or delete any request by selecting the down arrow.

If you prefer to delete all voice recordings you actually have to visit your Amazon account on the main Amazon website and find the **Manage Your Content and Devices** page of your account. Here is a direct link **www.amazon.com/mycd**

To find this page manually, go to **Amazon.com** and log in. Towards the top of the page to the right you will see **Account and Lists**. Hovering your mouse over this will reveal a large drop down menu and about half way down you will see **Your Content and**

Devices, click it. This is an incredibly useful and important page of your Amazon account for anything to do with the digital content you buy from Amazon, the electronic devices you have registered with Amazon and all associated settings. If we're ever unsure how to delete or change something in relation to our content and devices we inevitably find the answer on this page.

So returning to the question of how to delete all your voice recordings... once you are on the *Manage Your Content and Devices* page select the *Your Devices* tab.

Find *your Echo* and click the small box to the left. A popup window will appear with some options including Manage voice recordings. Keep in mind that Amazon Echo has been learning how you speak to give more consistently accurate answers. If you delete your voice recordings, you might find that the Echo's ability to understand you is reduced.

You'll have plenty of time to come back to the Home page later once you start using your Echo in earnest so we suggest you revisit the above information at a later date.

6. NOW PLAYING ON ECHO SHOW

You're not alone if you bought an Echo Show to enjoy its wide-ranging media content that includes music, movies, books and podcasts.

Well the **Now Playing** page is the page to come to when you are actually playing some of this content. Don't be concerned things like Music Unlimited and Playlists are mentioned in this chapter or anything else that you aren't familiar with, as you will be shortly. Feel free to read through this chapter and return to it later once you have some video or audio content actually playing.

When you're playing any form of entertainment, it appears on the **Now Playing** page along with its source. You can manage the audio with the Alexa app Media Player or directly on the Echo Show or using voice. Remember the Now Playing page on the mobile Alexa app is found by tapping the bottom right icon on the screen.

The Media Player on the **Now Playing** page has universal symbols:

- **Shuffle the Queue** of songs lined up to be played by selecting the crossed arrows on the left
- **Loop the Queue**, which means to play it continuously, by selecting the circling arrows on the right
- **Go back one song or skip the song** by using the Back/Forward symbols - solid arrows and line combinations
- **Play the song** by selecting the triangular arrow pointing right or pause the song with the side-by-side vertical lines
- **Adjust the Volume** by selecting the speaker symbol, grabbing the volume indicator and moving it up or down

If you have one of the several Amazon music accounts such as Prime or Unlimited, you'll have access to Stations and Playlists that can be played on Echo Show and will be shown on the Now Playing page.

When a Station or List is playing, you'll have **Thumbs Up** and **Thumbs Down** options in place of the **Shuffle** and **Loop** symbols. Amazon will monitor your preferences to customize the Station or List for you.

One function you can do on the **Echo Show screen** that you can't on the app is to rewind or fast-forward the song by touching and dragging the progress bar.

For voice, try requests like: *"Alexa...*

- *Shuffle"*
- *Pause"*
- *Repeat"*
- *Volume 8"*
- *Quieter"*
- *Skip"*
- *Thumbs up"* (for songs on custom Amazon Music stations)

The Now Playing page also shows your Queue and History.

Queue: This is the list of songs or other media that are lined up to be played in the Playlist or Station you've selected. We'll discuss specific music accounts much more in the next chapter. You can select any of the songs in the list for more options such as:

- Create a Station around the song or artist
- Add the song to your music library
- Shop for a digital version of the song or album on Amazon
- Rate the song with Thumbs Up or Thumbs Down (custom stations only)
- Select as a Favorite (some podcasts)

History: This list shows all the recent media you've played. Simply tap or select an item from the **History** list to enjoy it again. It will appear as what is Now Playing.

7. VIDEO

The next item on the menu is *Music, Video & Books*. Covering all three would make for a long chapter and would also make it difficult for readers of this guide to locate the information they wish to review. So, we'll take these entertainment options one at a time.

While Music is listed first in the tab title, Video options are shown first on the app. To maintain our systematic approach, let's start at the top of the page and work down over the next three chapters:

Chapter 7: Video

Chapter 8: Music

Chapter 9: Books

It's probable that Video is listed first because Amazon is aware of the ongoing growth in video media. The arrangement might also have been driven by Amazon's brief partnership with YouTube, which has ended for now. That doesn't mean that Alexa and YouTube won't partner again. Fingers crossed!

Amazon Video Options on Echo Show

Before we get to the two services shown on the Alexa app, let's discuss the immense amount of digital and streaming video available from Amazon. There are three primary ways to access video on Alexa and Echo Show:

- **Amazon Prime Video:** With an Amazon Prime or Prime for Students membership, you have access to thousands of movies, TV shows and original content from Amazon as part of your membership. Perhaps Amazon's movie and TV options aren't as wide ranging as Netflix, but Prime Video is part of the bigger Prime package that has a great many other benefits that Netflix and other streaming services don't have. If you're not a Prime member, choose **Try Prime** on Amazon.com to see all its benefits or to start your 30-day free trial.

- **Amazon Channels:** Premium channels like Showtime, HBO and Starz, plus niche genres for every age are available via monthly subscriptions once you have a Prime membership.

- **Amazon Video:** There's a wealth of digital movies, shows and other video content available from Amazon that can be purchased separately.

See what's available by hovering over Amazon Video in the Departments tab and choosing one of the options such as All Videos, Included with Prime or Amazon Channels. We've mentioned it before, but we've been Prime members for years, and think it is definitely worth the money.

Watching Video on Echo Show

When you've purchased video content, it is available in your Amazon account as **Your Video Library**. From there, you can add it to Your Watchlist of content you intend to watch soon.

Prime Video is available too. You can watch all options on your Echo Show. Available titles aren't stored on the app. You must request what you want to watch:

- **Not sure what to watch:** Say, *"Alexa, show my Watchlist,"* or *"Alexa, show my Video Library,"* and either will appear on the Show screen where you can browse by sliding left or watch by tapping your selection.

- **Want to see what's available in a genre:** Say, *"Alexa, show me comedy movies,"* or *"Alexa, show me TV shows."*

- **Want to see what's available from a favorite actor:** Say, *"Alexa, show me Gal Gadot movies,"* or *"Alexa, see movies with Benedict Cumberbatch."*

For the last two, Alexa will show options on the screen that you can browse. You will see the movie title, rating, whether closed captioning (CC) is available, year made, length and Purchase Options.

If you select **Purchase Options**, Alexa will say, "To watch [this movie], see your purchase options at Amazon.com slash video," which is **Amazon.com/video**.

If the content is free, you can select it, and it will begin to play.

When content is playing, here's how to control it:

- **Echo Show screen:** Tap the screen to display a limited player with a Pause/Play button and options to go back or forward 10 seconds. You can touch the progress bar to drag it forward or backward. The screen also shows a back arrow that can be tapped to go to the search results or to the last video played.

- **Voice:** Control the content with common voice commands like "*Alexa... Play/Pause/Resume*," or "*Rewind/fast forward*" any length of time. If you're watching a series, you can also say, "*Next video*" or "*next episode*."

Video content doesn't show on the **Now Playing** page. No Card is created.

Movie Trailers on Echo Show

Watch movie trailers from IMDB by saying, "*Alexa show me the movie trailer...*" for whatever trailer you want to see.

The trailer video can be controlled on the screen and with voice:

- **Echo Show screen:** Tap the screen, and use the pause/play buttons and 10-second rewind/fast forward buttons.

- **Voice:** Say, "*Play/Pause/Resume*," or "*Rewind/fast forward*" any length of time.

Note: Watching movie trailers on your Echo Show is a great little feature. Movie trailers are short, making them the perfect kind of video content to watch on the small screen of your Echo Show. We're not going to lie, not currently being able to watch similar short content from YouTube is disappointing. Being able to play movies and TV programs from Amazon is fine, but frankly why would you watch it on the small Echo Show screen when you can watch it on your TV? Hopefully we will see the return of YouTube to the Echo Show soon.

The best way to view Amazon Video is on your TV and for that we use Amazon's Fire TV discussed next.

Fire TV & Dish TV and the Alexa App

At this writing, Alexa works with Amazon Fire TV and Dish TV. Amazon has said the company is developing relationships with other video services, so expect this category to expand.

Amazon Fire TV

Fire TV is Amazon's streaming media player for your TV designed to improve your experience when accessing live content and streamed video, music and games. It's just like the Apple TV and Google's Chromecast. Some of the content is free but much of it requires a paid subscription. Fire TV equipment can be controlled with Alexa devices including the Echo Show.

Equipment: Currently you can buy the standard Fire TV unit, with or without an HD antenna, the Fire TV Stick & Alexa remote and a range of HDTV's with Fire TV built it. You can see the entire Fire TV family of devices here - **www.lyntons.com/FireTV**

Content: The stable of streaming and live TV subscription services is expanding rapidly and already includes Netflix, Hulu, Amazon, HBO Now, DirectTV Now, NBA, MLB, CNN,Crackle, ESPN, Showtime, Sling, Comedy Central, HGTV and AMC. You must have a subscription to these services for them to be available on Fire TV and controllable by Echo Show.

Setup and Use Fire TV with your Echo Show:

- Choose *Fire TV* from the *Video* section of *Music, Video, & Books*

- Select *Link Your Alexa Device* to choose which Fire TV equipment in the list you want to control with your Echo Show and Alexa

- Follow the prompts on the app to complete setup

Once setup is complete, you can access and control Fire TV content on your TV using your voice:

- Request the media you want to see or hear from free and subscription services by asking things like *"Alexa, search for Tom Cruise,"* or *"...search for action movies,"* or *"...search for Mission Impossible."* You can also open specific services by saying *"Alexa, open HBO Now"* etc.

- Once you're watching it, rewind or fast-forward streamed content for the length of time you choose using your voice and asking *"Alexa rewind 5 minutes,"* or *"...play next episode."*

Dish TV

Dish TV is one of the most popular satellite TV services available. Packages start at $49.99/month for the service. You must also lease the Hopper DVR for $10/month.

Equipment: Hopper DVR and any Echo device including Echo Show.

Information: Currently, Dish TV is offering new subscribers a free Amazon Echo Dot, the scaled-down version of the Echo that makes a nice secondary Echo device. All the details are at **Dish.com**.

Content: The company markets Dish as a cost-friendly alternative to cable that also provides 30 premium movie channels and more HD channels among its total 190 channels. Among the most popular channels are HBO, NFL Network, NFL RedZone, ESPN, Disney Channel, USA, ShowTime, Starz and Cinemax.

Setup and Use of Dish TV with Echo Show: Make sure popup windows are enabled on your browser. You might be asked to enter your Dish TV and Amazon login information during setup, so have it with you. Here are step-by-step linking instructions:

- Ensure that you have the latest version of the Hopper DVR software/firmware by going to channel 9607 on Dish TV and choosing *Software/Accessibility Update*

- If an update is needed, restart the Hopper when it is complete

- Choose *Dish TV* from the *Video* section of *Music, Video, & Books*

- Select *Enable Skill*

- Follow the prompts on the app to complete setup, which will include turning on the Hopper DVR and:

    1. Going to Menu

    2. Selecting *Settings*

    3. Selecting *Amazon Alexa*

    4. Selecting *Get Code*

    5. Entering the Code on the Alexa app where asked

    6. Selecting *Activate*

- Go to *Settings* on the Alexa app, choose *Hopper* from the list of discoverable devices and choose *Link Devices*

- Review the list of suggested things to say to control Dish TV with Echo Show such as "*Tune to ESPN*," and "*Pause Dish*." The use is very straightforward. Tell Alexa what you want, and you'll likely get it.

The connection should go smoothly. If you have issues, details for resolution might be found on the Dish TV Alexa integration page found here - **www.dish.com/AmazonAlexaIntegration**

Additional help on Quick Fixes for Alexa Video Skills is found on Amazon at - **www.lyntons.com/AVS**

Note that you will connect to a Fire TV by linking your Alexa device with your Fire TV account, but you connect to Dish TV by enabling the Skill. These are basically two ways of doing the same thing. Alexa skills - it's a growing range of diverse capabilities - are covered in the Skills section to follow.

8. MUSIC (AND LOTS MORE)

A world of music is available on your Echo Show, and it is delivered in multiple ways.

Some of the platforms discussed below also deliver news, sports, comedy, podcasts and more.

Building a music library may seem overwhelming.

If so, we suggest taking your time and having fun. Start with uploading some personal music you already have.

Then, incorporate music services you currently use, if any. From there, explore additional options one at a time.

A few have free accounts. The paid services offer 30-day free trials. Most are monthly subscriptions.

Even Amazon Prime has a monthly option, so there is no long-term commitment.

Just a heads-up at the beginning: We're going to talk about two related topics in this chapter, subscriptions to **Prime Music** and **Music Unlimited** and something called **Amazon Households**.

A Household is formed by linking two separate Amazon accounts to Alexa with one benefit being the ability to listen to each other's Library of music.

Subscriptions and Households are **both OPTIONAL**.

If you want to learn Echo Show basics right now and consider options later, you won't miss anything essential if you gloss over these sections. Come back to them if or when you have an interest in them.

In this chapter we will take you through each music page, explaining what you can do on each page and what each service provides, how to set them up and how to control them with your voice or the Alexa App.

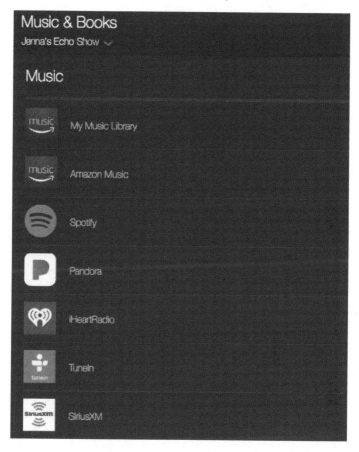

My Music Library

The first page in the music section of *Music, Video & Books* on your Alexa app is *My Music Library*. Under the My Music Library heading, you MIGHT see:

- **Whose Device or App:** If you have more than one Echo device or smart device connected to this Amazon account, they will all be listed here, and you can choose the one you want to listen to music on, such as Jenna's Echo Show or Tom's Echo in our case. If your Echo Show is the only device, then another option you might see is...

- **Whose Library:** This is the name of the Library you're viewing such as Jenna's Library. The reason the library is identified is because Amazon allows Alexa users to create an Amazon Household to share their music libraries (and more). If interested, you can learn more by going to the **Manage Your Household** page where you can create a Household by supplying login information and profiles for:

  1. Up to 2 adults

  2. Up to 4 teens 13-17

  3. Up to 4 children up to 12

Amazon isn't strict about Household members being relatives, but it will know people's ages that already have an Amazon account. Everyone in an Amazon Household can listen to one another's libraries.

Below these two possible options you will see the main contents of your Music Library which will comprise of music that you have:

- Already purchased on Amazon.com
- Uploaded to your Amazon Music account from your pc or mac computer
- Selected from your Prime Music or Music Unlimited subscriptions if you have either.

We will discuss **Prime Music** and **Music Unlimited** subscriptions in the next section of this chapter. And not much more needs to be said about music you have already purchased.

Any music you've already bought from Amazon will automatically appear here in **My Music Library** and you just have to click or tap any track that you see here while using the Alexa App to start it playing.

And of course the whole point of Alexa is to operate it/her with your voice, so you can also start a track playing by saying "**Alexa play Can't Stop the Feeling by Justin Timberlake**," or the name of a track, album or artist that you have previously purchased.

Finding/viewing the music you would like to listen to in your **Music Library** is quite straightforward.

Search your Library: This search box is a quick way to find an Artist, Album or Song. The search results list will begin populating as you type.

Playlists, Artists, Albums, Songs, Genres: My Music Library is divided into these five categories. Select any of them, and all available options will be shown. The A through Z list that appears in each category, except Playlists, allows you to quickly search for something in the list, reducing the scrolling required.

Upload Music to My Music Library

As mentioned, music that you upload from your home computer (PC or Mac) will also appear here in the **My Music Library** section of the Alexa App.

This feature, the ability to transfer music from your computer to your Amazon account, is especially useful for those of us who have purchased lots of music from Itunes or Google Play.

As we talked about in **Chapter 2** you can play your iTunes collection on the Echo by connecting your mobile device (phone or tablet) via Bluetooth.

This requires you to choose and start playing your music via your mobile device first.

Yes, you can then use voice commands to pause or resume a track and skip forward or back to other tracks etc, and if you're happy with this arrangement then we suggest you stick with it.

However this method does slightly ignore the main benefit of owning an Echo, namely the ability to control all your music entertainment with your voice alone.

If all you want to do is stream music from your phone to a speaker in your home then you could have bought any Bluetooth speaker and, indeed, one that has better sound quality!

Our preferred solution is to upload our most listened to music from our iTunes collection to our Amazon music account/library so that we have complete vocal control over it, without having to touch any other device.

Amazon allows you to add 250 tracks that you have bought from other stores for free, that's not a whole lot of music, but it's enough to make sure we always have our most loved music to hand.

If you want to upload more music, or your entire collection, then you can buy extra storage space from Amazon for $24.99 a year.

For that price you can upload 250,000 songs and if that's not enough music then you might want to talk to somebody about your music addiction! ;-)

Visit this page for more information - **www.lyntons.com/storage**

To upload music you will need to install the Amazon Music App on your Mac or PC. This app is Amazon's equivalent of iTunes.

These are the steps you need to take to upload music currently in iTunes on your computer to your Amazon Music Library.

1. Go to **music.amazon.com** and sign in with your Amazon account details.

2. Scroll down the left sidebar until you see *Upload your music* and click on it.

3. A box will appear prompting you to download the Amazon Music App, go ahead and download the app.

4. When the app has finished downloading open it and sign in again with your Amazon account details. Just so you know, now that you have the Amazon Music app you can always use it, just like iTunes, to play all your Amazon music on your computer if you wish.

5. Once the app is open, look to the right and you will see under **Actions** three boxes and the one you are interested in is *"Upload: Drag and drop"*

6. Now open iTunes and, depending on which music you want to upload, click on *Artists, Albums* or *Songs* to bring up your music.

7. Now simply click and hold on the music you want to upload

and drag it out of Itunes and into the *"Upload: Drag and drop"* box in your Amazon Music app

And that's it, your selection will start uploading to your Amazon Music account and the app will notify you when uploading is complete.

We recommend when doing this that you resize the two app windows, iTunes and Amazon Music, so that they are smaller and you can see both clearly on your computer screen. This will make dragging and dropping files much easier.

Amazon Music: What it Offers

There's a long list of benefits for using Amazon Prime including Prime Music. There's a 30-day free trial here - **www.lyntons.com/ usprime** - if you want to try it out before making a commitment.

With Prime Music you have unlimited ad-free access to more than two million songs in addition to complete albums and stations created for all major music genres. If you're not interested in Amazon Prime then rest assured there are plenty of other free music options available that we discuss later in this chapter.

Amazon are now offering a further music subscription called **Amazon Music Unlimited**, for a monthly subscription fee you can listen to even more music via your Echo.

If you would like to know more visit this page - **www.lyntons.com/ Amusic**. Personally we find that the music options offered via our Prime membership is sufficient for our needs.

Exploring Your Prime Music Account

Once you've joined Amazon Prime you can return to the Alexa App and click on *Music, Video & Books > Amazon Music* and start to explore your options.

It would be an understatement to say that there are a lot of musical options on the Amazon Music homepage. Frankly, there are so many options, and so many of them overlap, that it was initially confusing.

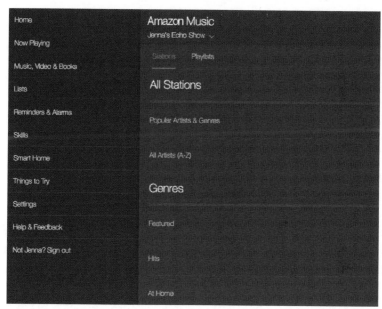

Think of it this way: The Amazon Music categories discussed below attempt to organize the entire catalog of modern music into logical groups which Amazon term as **Stations** and **Playlists.** There aren't hard and fast distinctions between these groups.

We quickly realized that there are just too many options to get a handle on easily so we adopted an adventurous, open-minded attitude.

We pick a station or playlist that sounds good to us, and wait to hear what songs are included in the collection. We then note the station and return to it or avoid it based on our tastes.

Okay, with that perspective in mind, here is an overview of the musical groupings. Take a relaxed hour or so to explore what's available and get a feel for what directions you want to explore first.

Prime Stations

The dozens of stations cover all the musical styles we're familiar with, and we're music buffs, plus lots we're not acquainted with but look forward to exploring.

Here's something we didn't expect when we began to listen: Stations named for a specific artist play that artist as well as similar artists. For example, the James Taylor station plays plenty of JT, of course, but also Christopher Cross, Joni Mitchell, Jim Croce, Gordon Lightfoot, Carole King, Jackson Browne, etc.

All Stations: The first thing you will see when you click on Stations within the **Amazon Music** page on the Alexa App is the *All Stations* heading and below that *Popular Artists & Genres* and *All Artists*.

The next heading is *Genres* which are divided into favorites such as Alternative, Blues, Children's Music, Classical, Classic Rock, Decades, Gospel and Pop. Each genre offers stations named for artists, decades and styles.

The *All Artists* list is sorted from A-Z but there is no way to search the list, you just have to scroll, scroll, scroll down an immensely long list of artists. We've found this to be frustrating, we're interested to discover new artists but we'd like more to go on than just a name we've not heard of!

The *Genres* section makes much more sense for those who know what they like and don't want to wade through an ocean of music that doesn't suit their tastes. Selecting any of the genres will lead to a list of sub-genres, only proving that an immense amount of music is available through these music services.

Prime Playlists

There are thousands of Playlists that give you a more specific slice of the types of music you like, and your options are incredibly diverse. You can search Playlists by **Mood & Activities, Genres, Artists** and **Decades** to locate those that appeal to you. Select "**Add Playlist to Library**" and the list will be transferred and stored in **My Music Library** to be played on your Echo Show, phone or other device using the Alexa App and/or your voice.

When we clicked into **Mood & Activities** we didn't have to go further than **Happy & Upbeat** to find a whole bunch of playlists that we love!

See what we mean? Amazon Prime offers a torrent of music, and there are innumerable places to jump into the rushing waters. We think you'll enjoy the ride, as we do.

Top Tip: On the **Now Playing** Page, when any track is playing from a Prime Station or Playlist you can save it to your **Music Library**. Find the track to the right of the **Now Playing** page under **Queue**, click the small down arrow and then click **Add this song to your library**.

BUT what if you want to listen to the entire album that a track was taken from? Playlists or Stations with a selection of tracks, all from different albums, is great but sometimes you just want to hear one specific album from beginning to end.

For the moment Amazon doesn't always make it easy to save a whole album via the Alexa App so here's our workaround...

Let's take the track "Happy" by Pharrell Williams which we came across in one of our Happy & Upbeat Prime Playlists. When the track is playing we can see on the Now Playing page of the Alexa App that the song is taken from the album G I R L. Now we go to **Amazon.com** and type "**G I R L by Pharrell Williams**" into the search box and straight away we can see the album cover and details including a **Listen Now** tab indicating that this album is free for us to listen to as Prime members.

Clicking on the **Listen Now** tab instantly opens the Amazon Music app in a new browser window and the album starts playing through our pc speakers. Under the album title, as well as a pause button you will see a box saying "**+ Add to My Music**". When you click that box the album is immediately added to My Music Library and now all I have to do to hear that album in its entirety is say "**Alexa play G-I-R-L by Pharrell Williams**," and... the album starts playing via my Echo Show!

Note: We've found that this whole process is a lot easier when listening to a Prime Station, as opposed to a Playlist. When playing a Station go to the **Now Playing** page and under **Queue**, click the small down arrow and as well as **Add this song to your library** you should also see the option **View album in Prime Music**. Click or tap here to go directly to the album page on Amazon and then follow the instructions above to add it to your library.

Controlling Prime Music with Your Echo and App

Using voice, it is as easy as saying, "**Alexa, play 50 Great Happy Songs**," to get the music started. The Echo Show will reply with "The Playlist 50 Great Happy Songs from Amazon Music," and a great selection of happy toe tapping music will fill the air through the Echo's quality speaker. Once the chosen list is playing, Alexa will respond to commands that control the music. These include, "**Alexa...**

- **What's playing?"**
- **Turn it up or Softer "**
- **Volume 5"**
- **Skip or Next Song"**
- **Pause, Resume or Continue"**
- **Loop"**
- **Stop"**
- **Continue"**
- **Add this song"** (to your Music Library)

When using the Alexa App instead of your voice, simple taps or clicks are all that are needed to choose the music you want to play. When you've made your choice, a player appears with options for play, pause, skip ahead, go back or shuffle the music.

Spotify: What it Offers

This Swedish streaming service hooked up with Alexa after iHeartRadio and several others were onboard.

In similar fashion, Spotify delivers music (30 million songs and counting) and podcasts to Echo Show users through searchable artists, albums, labels, genres and playlists.

While Spotify has both Free and Premium subscriptions, you'll need to go with Premium to listen to the service using Alexa.

The current cost for Spotify Premium is $9.99, but a 30-day free trial is available that gives you ad-free streaming, unlimited skips and play any track features.

Of course you can use a Spotify free account with your Echo Show too. Remember that you can connect your mobile phone to your Echo via Bluetooth.

When you do this, whatever you play on your phone, including music playing in the Spotify app, will play through your Amazon Echo Show speakers. Not the perfect Alexa integrated solution, but certainly a budget workaround.

Setting Up Your Spotify Account

Go to **www.spotify.com**, click *Get Spotify Premium* and sign up. Once you've established a Spotify account, synching it to the Alexa App on your laptop or phone will take just a couple of minutes.

Go back into the Alexa App, go to *Music, Video & Books > Spotify* and click *Link your account*. You'll then be taken back to the Spotify website to authorize the connection between Alexa and Spotify.

It's that simple. Back on the Spotify page of your Alexa App you'll be asked whether you want to make Spotify your default music library. Hold fire on that for a moment as, we're about to explain how to operate Spotify with your Echo Show next.

Controlling Spotify with Your Voice and App

Using voice commands: Speaking directly to the Echo Show or using the Alexa remote, ask, *"Alexa, play Twenty One Pilots on Spotify."* It's important to include *"on Spotify"* or Alexa will try to select music from your Amazon Music library first. That is unless you make Spotify your default music service!

If you believe that you will be using Spotify to play the majority of your music on your Echo Show then setting Spotify as your default music library makes sense.

With this service set as default you can ask for music without specifying Spotify, Alexa will automatically look to play a music choice via Spotify rather than anywhere else.

Of course if you choose this setting you will now have to specify Amazon Music by name if you want the Echo Show to play something from that library.

To set Spotify as your default music library go to *Settings* in the Alexa App then scroll down and click the *Choose default music services* box. Then choose *Spotify* under *Default music library* and finally click *Done*

When requesting music from Spotify you can ask for a specific song name, playlist name, genre, artist, composer or Discover Weekly to hear what's new. For example, say, *"Alexa, play songs by Carrie Underwood on Spotify,"* or *"Alexa, play Work by Rihanna on Spotify."*

Command options are what you'd expect: Pause, resume, stop, mute, previous, next, shuffle, skip this song, volume 1-10, volume up/down, etc. Remember to use your wake word.

You can get answers to questions like, *"Alexa, what song is playing?"* and *"who is this artist?"*

Using the Alexa App: Use the **Now Playing** page to view the current Spotify music you're listening to and use standard command options such as play, pause, skip, previous, next and shuffle.

Unlinking Spotify and Amazon Accounts

If you don't want the accounts linked:

- Open the Alexa App
- Browse the Menu, and choose *Settings*
- Choose *Music & Media*
- Choose *Spotify* from the list
- Choose *Unlink* account from Alexa
- Choose the *Unlink* option

Pandora: What it Offers

pandora®

Pandora offers hundreds of customized stations in more than 40 genres. There are standards such as Blues, Classical and Comedy and quite a few unique offerings like BBQ, Festivals and Musica Romantica.

Setting Up Your Pandora Account

Select the Pandora tab from within *Music, Video & Books* to get started. You'll have the option of signing in to an existing Pandora account or registering a new one. A new account requires providing your email, user name, password, gender and zip code.

Once you've signed in or created an account, Pandora is immediately supported by Alexa. For those with an existing account, your stations will appear in My Stations, and you can alter or delete them as you wish.

Pandora Basic is free, but short commercials occasionally play between tracks. An upgrade to a Pandora Plus account is available on the Pandora site. A Pandora Plus account is ad free and allows more song skips. Currently, the upgrade is $4.99 per month.

You can use this link to upgrade - **www.pandora.com/upgrade**

Controlling Pandora With Your Voice and App

If you've created a new Pandora account, start by selecting the +*Create Station* box at the top of the Pandora page on the Alexa App. From there, you can use the box to search for an artist, genre or track, or you can see what's already available in the Browse Genre section.

When you select an existing station, it begins to play and also appears in the list entitled My Stations on the Pandora Page in the Alexa App.

Select the down arrow to have the option of deleting the station. Pandora allows you to create up to 100 of your own stations to supplement what is already available. For example, we're fans of a musical genre called reggaeton, and there's not a pre-existing station for it.

However, when we typed reggaeton into the search box, several tracks came up. We selected the track Reggaeton Latino, and a station was created with that tune and similar songs.

We spell this out in detail because there are no "how-to's" given on the app. Some tasks, such as creating our own stations, we learned how to do through trial and error.

However, as far as stations are concerned, there are already so many customizable stations within each genre of music, creating your own might not be something you'll want to do anyway.

Any station's playlist can be customized by eliminating unwanted songs from the list. Do this by saying, *"Alexa, thumbs down,"* or by selecting the downward pointing thumb on the player at the bottom of the Alexa App.

Note, however, you'll only be able to delete or skip three songs on any list. The fourth attempt will produce a drop-down menu saying, "Our music licenses limit the number of songs you may skip." In other words, you'll have to listen to the remaining songs all the way through or choose a new station to play.

As ever the player bar at the bottom of the Alexa App offers options to play, pause, go forward and go back. If you click or tap the small icon of the album cover for the song playing, you'll get the full **Now Playing** page view with a larger icon and a list of the songs as they play.

You'll also have the option here to look at your stations history and the queue of songs that have played on the current station. Choose the down arrow of any of the songs in the queue to rate it, create a song or artist station, shop for the music at the Amazon Digital Store, Bookmark the song or give the song a rest by selecting "*I'm tired of this track*."

You can use voice commands with Pandora on the Echo Show, just as you can with other services.

If you want to control content from Pandora with your voice, and we're sure you will, we highly recommend that you choose and add Pandora Stations via the Alexa App first.

We drove ourselves crazy and had a good few laughs trying to get Alexa to play a station if we hadn't already added it via the Alexa App. You can make Pandora the default station service for the Echo Show but even doing that didn't seem to help much when requesting a station that we hadn't previously saved.

If you don't believe us try asking "*Alexa play GameDay Rap and Hip Hop Radio on Pandora*" and see what you get if you haven't already added that station to your favorite Stations! It seems that once you have chosen a station and played it once then Alexa is able to recognize what you're saying the next time you ask.

We didn't find making Pandora our default station service particularly helpful but if you want to try go to **Settings > Music & Media**, scroll down and click the ***Choose default music services*** box. Then choose ***Pandora*** under ***Default station service*** and finally click ***Done***

iHeartRadio: What it Offers

This network is a digital radio and content streaming service that includes thousands of live radio stations and podcasts from the US. iHeartRadio gives you the option to create personalized **Custom Stations** featuring your favorite artists or genre.

Music is just the beginning. Other categories include **Business & Finance, Comedy, Entertainment, Food, Games & Hobbies, Health, News, Politics, Science, Spirituality** and **Sports**.

Each group offer numerous and wide-ranging options, so it will take you some time to explore what's available and find shows you want to return to often.

We've setup iHeartRadio as our default station service because it offers both curated music playlists, just like Pandora, and real radio stations, just like TuneIn (see below); so two for the price of one.

Setting Up Your iHeartRadio Account

To enjoy iHeartRadio on your Echo Show, no account is necessary. Simply use the Alexa App to explore and listen. However, with an account, you can create Custom Stations and share them with others.

Select iHeartRadio on the Alexa App and then click "**Link your account now**" to be taken to a special sign in/sign up page for activating you iHeartRadio with your Echo.

If you don't have an account, set one up using an email address and password. You'll also be asked to provide zip code, gender and agreement with the site's Terms of Service. Another option is to link an existing Facebook or Google Plus account to create an iHeartRadio account.

Controlling iHeartRadio With Your Voice and App

When using the Alexa app click or tap the *iHeartRadio* tab within *Music, Films & Books* and your options appear in the main screen. They include Search for artist or station, Browse for Favorites you've chosen while using the network.

The Browse option gives choices for Live Radio, Perfect For (Kids, Working Out, Driving and more), iHeartRadio Originals and Shows. We had a lot of fun exploring the variety of choices available.

The Originals tab features dozens of unique stations including Golden Era musical numbers, Sippy Cup for pre-schoolers, Classical Genius featuring Mozart and his contemporaries, Workout Beats, All 60s, Road Trip and Chillax.

To use voice commands to play iHeartRadio, you have to know the name of the show, station or radio program you want to listen to.

When requesting a radio station, your best bet to get it working is to refer to it with the exact title of the station as it is shown in the Alexa App.

Some use call letters; others use a name such as The Bear or Kat Country.

We had to experiment in order to access some stations. For example, we requested the station listed as New Country 96.3 KSCS.

When we asked for it by "*New Country*" the Echo retrieved a top country hits station from Amazon Prime Music. We then asked for *"KSCS 96.3,"* and the radio station was properly accessed.

TuneIn: What it Offers

TuneIn is completely free, and setting up an account isn't necessary. However, having an account allows you to "Follow" your favorite stations and shows and to Share them on Facebook, Twitter and Google Plus and Tumblr.

On TuneIn, you've got the opportunity to access more than 100,000 Internet radio stations including FM, AM, HD, LP and digital. Brands featured include ESPN, NPR, Public Radio International, CBS and C-Span. Your browsing options include much more than music.

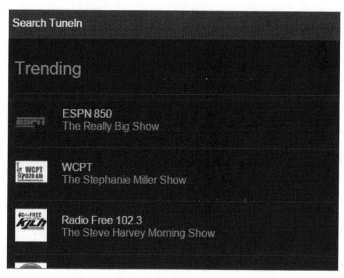

There is Local Radio, Sports, News, Talk and by Location along with popular shows featured in all of those genres. There are more than 4 million podcasts, concerts and interviews available too, a fact that sets TuneIn apart from its competitors.

TuneIn is great but we prefer to use it on our cell phones when we're out and about and prefer iHeartRadio for our Echo Show.

Setting Up Your TuneIn Account

As mentioned there's no need to set anything up to use TuneIn, you can access and browse everything on offer by following the instructions below.

However, if you do want to take advantage of some further features you can join TuneIn at **tunein.com**. Signing up is a brief procedure that includes choosing a user name with an associated email address and a password. You also have the option of signing in with an existing Facebook or Google+ account, a step that simplifies accessing a new or existing account.

Once you have an account you can create and organize a library of your preferred categories, songs and artists that can be accessed and played on your Echo Show using voice or the app. Similar to Prime Music, there is a massive amount of content to explore on TuneIn, so enjoy the process of discovery!

Controlling TuneIn With Your Voice and App

If you know the radio station name or station call sign or the name of the podcast, you can use voice commands to get exactly what you want. However, you need to be really precise with the correct name of the station and even then we have had problems.

We had no problems asking "*Alexa, play Mix 90's on TuneIn,*" but we couldn't for the life of us get "*Alexa, play The Bear 98.1 on TuneIn*" to work. In the end we had to use this work around...

If you can't get Alexa to recognize a TuneIn radio station name that you are asking for, then instead start playing it manually by clicking or tapping on your chosen station via the TuneIn page in your Alexa App. Then once the station is playing go to the **Now Playing** page.

On the Now Playing page, to the right you will see your selected station and a small down arrow (it's called a caret apparently). Click the arrow and the click on Favorite station to save it as a favorite. It was only after we had saved The Bear 98.1 as a favorite that we could ask "*Alexa play The Bear 98.1 on TuneIn*" and have her play the station.

Using Tunein with the Alexa app: The Tunein page within *Music, Video & Books* is very simple to navigate:

Use the Search Box to learn what's available related to your search word. You'll receive unsorted results that take time to scroll through, but if you're just browsing, you might not mind that. If you want a specific station or national network, type in call letters such as *WABC* or the name of the network such as *NPR* or *Foxnews*.

Browse the categories listed beneath the search box starting with stations you have selected as a Favorite. Local Radio options will be given based on the address you supplied when setting up your Echo Show. That can be changed in the app *Settings* by choosing *your Echo Show* from the device list, scrolling down to *Device Location* and using the *Edit* option. Selecting any of the genres listed will open a list of sub-genres and Stations for you to consider.

We find it easier to play content from TuneIn using the Alexa App on our mobile phones.

SiriusXM: What it Offers

One of the first satellite radio services, SiriusXM now offers streaming Internet radio to compete with iHeartRadio and Tunein.

It offers more than 120 channels covering music, news, talk, entertainment and sports plus niche stations like comedy and Latin interests.

Setting Up Your SiriusXM Account

SiriusXM is a Skill, which means that the service can be used with Alexa and your Echo Show, but isn't supported to the extent Spotify, Tunein and the others are. We have a **chapter on Skills** later, but basically they're third-party services that can be linked with Alexa and used with functionality that might be limited, and that's the case with SiriusXM. A quick click on the Skills section in the app will show you how diverse Alexa Skills are.

All Skills are rated by Alexa users with comments that will help you decide whether to try it or not. The average Skill rating is 3 to 3.5 stars, and SiriusXM is a 3-star skill presently after almost 1,400 reviews. What's playing isn't displayed on Echo Show, and SiriusXM sometimes doesn't recognize login information. Some users report the connection is intermittent. If you have SiriusXM already, try the Skill, rate it and let other Echo users know what you think. That's part of the fun of using Skills.

OK, here's how to use SiriusXM with Alexa on your Echo Show:

- Go to **SiriusXM.com/amazonalexa**
- If you have SiriusXM, select the *Set Me Up to Stream* option, and follow the brief instructions on linking your account to Alexa
- If you don't have the service, start a free trial to one of the packages:

    1. **80 Channels called Mostly Music:** $10.99/month

    2. **140 Channels called XM Select:** $15.99

    3. **150+ Channels including Howard Stern called XM All Access:** $19.99/month

- If a new subscriber, open the confirmation email from SiriusXM, and select the link to set up your account

- Log in to SiriusXM when prompted

- Open the SiriusXM tab on the Alexa app

- Enable the Skill, and follow the instructions for linking the account, which might appear in a pop-up window depending on what device you're using the app with.

Controlling SiriusXM With Your Voice and App

Hopefully by now you get the gist of how to operate all these different music services and SiriusXM is no different. Once your account is linked with Alexa you can use your voice to start content playing via your Echo Show.

Either ask *"Alexa, play (name of station),"* or *"Alexa, play channel (station channel number)."*

Full disclosure... we don't use this service and the number of bad reviews for this skill, as well as the added cost, has put us off trying it.

9. BOOKS

We're never short on things to read or books to listen to using Echo Show. The two services available, Audible and Kindle Books have impressive libraries of reading material. Let's explore them!

Audible

Listening to books used to be a quirky thing people with long commutes did. Now, the concept is trending and expanding beyond books with a plethora of podcasts (free with a Prime subscription) plus original content created to be read like a radio drama. We listen to Audible about three times a week, usually to relax in the evening or while getting cozy on a rainy weekend afternoon.

Audible is owned by Amazon, and the company has invested significant dollars in developing content.

Account details:

- $14.95/month after 30-day free trial
- Trial includes one book to keep free, stored in Your Audiobooks library in the app
- 180,000 titles with more added every day
- Many free titles with Amazon, and you can select as many as you like
- Subscription includes one book per month of your choice, and you are given a few days to try the book and exchange it if you don't like it

- 30% discount on additional books
- You have 12 months to return "a set number of books" you don't like, according to Amazon
- Listen on any Echo device, and control the content with the Player on the Alexa app
- Listen on your smart phone or device using the Audible app
- Use the Whispersync app to listen and keep track of where you are in the book on all your devices

Setting Up Your Audible Account

To set up your Audible account go to **www.audible.com**

- Create an account, and start your free trial
- You will be taken to your Amazon account to sign in
- Select the existing payment method shown by the last 4 numbers or enter a new payment method
- Start your membership, and pick your free book
- Mark your calendar, so you'll remember to cancel within 30 days if you don't want to keep Audible

Connecting Audible and Alexa:

- Choose **Audible** from the **Books** section in the Alexa app
- Choose **Link Account**, and follow the brief instructions
- Your Audible book or books will appear in the Your Audiobooks list
- Download the Audible app to your smart devices - available on Google Play and iTunes

Controlling Audible With Your Echo and App

- Manually choose the book you want from Your Audiobooks library or say, "*Alexa, read The Magic of Thinking Big*"
- For books previously begun, say "*Alexa, resume The Magic of Thinking Big*," and it will pick up where you left off

- The book will appear on Echo Show, on the Now Playing page and on the small player at the bottom of any page when viewing the app online
- Manually select a chapter on the Player or verbally request the chapter you want
- Use the Player to go back or forward 30 seconds, pause or play and change the volume
- Use verbal requests like *"go back two minutes,"* or *"go to the next chapter."*
- Request Alexa to *"stop reading in 10 minutes,"* or *"set a sleep timer for 10 minutes."*

Kindle Books: What it Offers

Kindle has dominated the eBook market for a decade, and now Alexa can read many of your favorites with hands-free ease.

Account details:

- You can buy individual titles without a subscription by choosing the Kindle version when purchasing a book
- Your second option is a Kindle Unlimited subscription for $9.99/month with unlimited access to one million books and magazines, though few are new or recently released books
- A six-month subscription is available for $59.94
- Amazon Prime members get one early release book called a Kindle First plus one additional book free each month
- Read books in the Library of your Amazon Household members (for more info go to the *Accounts & Lists* tab on Amazon.com and select *Amazon Household* in the *Shopping Programs and Rentals* section)

- You have the option to borrow and lend books with other Kindle users and rent textbooks too

Personally we're not fans of Kindle Unlimited, we tend to buy books by well-known established authors and rarely find their books included in the subscription. Furthermore, while we like this audio feature on Alexa, the books are read in Alexa's computerized voice which is a poor substitute for a professionally recorded audio book.

Setting Up Kindle Books Audio

- No account is needed to buy individual books
- If you're a Prime member, you already have a Kindle First plus one additional book free each month, and it can be accessed from the **Accounts & Lists** drop-down menu on Amazon.com
- If you already have a Kindle account, your Kindle books will appear in your Kindle Library on the Alexa app
- For a 30-day trial to Kindle Unlimited, go to **Amazon.com/ kindleunlimited** or type **Kindle Unlimited** in the Amazon search box
- Choose **Start your 30-day Free Trial**
- Sign into your Amazon account
- Choose an existing payment method or enter a new one
- Start your membership, and enjoy browsing for titles that interest you
- Books you buy, borrow or rent will show up in the Alexa App
- Mark your calendar, so you'll remember to cancel within 30 days, if you wish

Controlling Kindle With Your Echo and App

Since Kindle is an Amazon service, it's already connected to Alexa. Choose **Kindle Books** in the Alexa app, and your available books should be ready to enjoy. Books are read in Alexa's voice.

- Manually choose a book from the list called **Books Alexa Can Read**, and it will start

- Control it on the **Now Playing** page of the Alexa app including selecting the chapter you want from the **Queue**, changing the volume, pausing it or going back or forward 30 seconds

- Optionally use your voice to request a title, a chapter of the book currently being read, or say, "**Alexa, read a Kindle book**," and Alexa will ask for the title you want to hear

- Once the book is being read, you can say things like, "**Alexa, go back three minutes**," "**Alexa, stop reading in 10 minutes**," or "**Alexa, set a 10-minute sleep timer**" to stop the reading when you choose

- If you've started a book previously, Alexa will start where you left off

Audiobook Immersion Reading

We wonder whether this concept will catch on. Immersion reading is listening to a book being read while viewing the text. The text is highlighted as it is read.

Amazon suggests that immersion reading creates a deeper connection with the book. We've tried it, but found it oddly difficult to read and listen at the same time, even to the same text. If you're curious and want to learn more or try immersion reading, visit **audible.com/ mt/immersion**.

10. LISTS

Amazon first envisioned Echo devices as virtual personal assistants, and this remains a significant part of their core identity. The Alexa app and Echo Show work well together in helping us assemble, view and manage our Shopping List and To-do List on a daily basis, and we're sure they'll do the same for you.

The Echo personal assistant does a pretty good job populating the list via voice commands, though it might get a word wrong here or there. We asked, "*Alexa, add 'find CDs' to my to-do list*," and what appeared on the list was, "**Find c.d.s**". Then, a note to get "**screen grabs**" was listed as "**screen grahams**". Misunderstandings happen most often with uncommon words.

There have been occasions where we've had to cast our minds back and remember what it was we asked Alexa to add because what's on the list doesn't make sense. It's inspired a blend of comedy, frustration and "ah-ha!" moments when we figure it out.

Typically, a request such as, "*Alexa, add mow the grass to the to-do list*," is clearly understood. Amazon suggests as an alternate saying something like, "*Alexa, I need to organize my tools*". We've found that the Echo doesn't comprehend this voice command very well. We stick to the "*Alexa add (something) to my to-do list*" commands for best results.

Select **Lists** in the Menu where you will see your **Shopping List**. The heading next to it is your **To-do List**. Manually manage the lists by clicking/tapping back and forth between them.

Shopping List

Creating a shopping list has never been so easy. Add items as the need arises, and you'll have a list you can print or take with you to the store on your mobile device.

We haven't shopped from a paper list since buying our first Amazon Echo several years ago. Our list is right there on our phone, and using the app, we can also compare prices at Amazon for major items we're looking at in the store.

Create and add to your list in two ways:

- **On the app:** Type what you need into the ***Add Item*** box, and select the + sign or hit ***Enter***, and it will be added.

- **Using voice:** Tell Alexa to add what you want to the Shopping List, and she'll tell you it was added. The Shopping List will appear on the Echo Show screen with the newly added item. Alexa will add doubles of things, if you ask for it twice. That's a minor issue easily remedied. Removing items is discussed below.

When using Alexa on your computer, choose the ***Print*** option, and your computer's **Print Manager** will open.

Review your Shopping List: Check it any time on your computer or device using the app. Say, "***Alexa, shopping list***," and Alexa will read the list to you, and it will appear on the Echo Show screen. Say "***Alexa, show me the shopping list***," and it will appear without Alexa reading it. One of us prefers to read it; the other prefers listening to it while doing other tasks.

Manage your Shopping List in these ways:

- **On the app:** Check off items by selecting the box. Select ***Delete*** to remove them immediately, which we do when we mistakenly add something a second time, or they will be transferred to the **Completed** list when you navigate away from the Shopping List. Select the down arrow for these options:

1. **Search Amazon** for tahini (more about online shopping later)

2. **Search Bing** for tahini

3. **Move item to To-do List** (If you say, *"Alexa, add clean the windows to the list,"* Alexa might add it to your Shopping List. Be sure to specify the To-do list for that sort of thing.)

4. **Delete Item** to remove something from the list

The list on the app shows the Active list, that is, things not yet checked off. You can view checked-off items by selecting **View Completed** at the top of the page. There, you can also delete checked off items individually or all at once.

- **On Your Echo Show:** Say, *"Alexa, show me the shopping list,"* or similar request, and it will appear on the screen. To remove an item:

    1. Swipe left, and it will be gone

    2. Tap it, select the "***X***" next to the item name, and tap the ***Done*** button.

If Alexa misheard you, the wrong item will be listed. Tap the screen and use the keypad to make the correction, much as you would when correcting text on your phone. As you're typing in the correct item, suggestions will appear that you can tap to select.

- **Using voice:** When the Shopping List is displayed on the Echo Show screen say, *"Alexa, remove item five from shopping list,"* or *"remove fresh vegetables from the list."* If the list isn't being displayed on the Show and you ask this, Alexa will give verbal instructions for manually checking off an item.

A Card is created on the app **Home** page when you add an item to the Shopping List. Options on the Card include **View Shopping List** (and you'll be taken to it) and the same shopping options available on the List such as searching Amazon or Bing for the item.

How we use the Shopping List: The great thing about these options is that we can compile a single list using multiple forms of input.

If we're going through the refrigerator or the pantry, it's easiest to verbally list items.

However, we suggest listing them one at a time. For example, it's easier to say, "*Alexa, add romaine lettuce, red peppers and kale to the Shopping List*," but then they all appear as one item, not three. When shopping, we prefer each item listed separately to avoid overlooking something.

When we're away from the Echo Show, adding items to the list via our phone or laptop is very easy. Frankly, if you're a fast typist, you might be able to add a bunch of items to your list manually faster than you can using voice to mention an item, wait for Alexa to respond, mention an item, wait... and so on.

To-do List

It's just as easy to create and manage a To-do list. The process is much the same.

Create a To-do list: You can start a list and add to it in two ways:

- **On the app:** When you select the *Lists* tab on the app, your Shopping list will appear. Choose the *To-do* tab next to the Shopping heading, type the task into the *Add Item* box, and add it by selecting the + sign or pressing the *Enter key*.

- **Using voice:** Say, "*Alexa, add reserve meeting room to my to-do list*." Alexa will let you know the task has been added.

Review your To-do List: Select the *To-do* tab on your Lists page or ask Alexa to "*read*" your list to hear and see it or "*show*" your list to see it without narration. If you simply say, "*Alexa, To-do list*," Alexa will ask, "What shall I add to your To-do list."

Manage your To-do List in two convenient ways:

On the App: Select back and forth between the **Active** list of uncompleted tasks and the **Completed** list of checked tasks. **On the Active list:**

- Check off items by selecting the box, and a check-mark will appear
- Delete checked items immediately, if you want to remove it
- **View more options:** Select the task itself, not the check box, to Move item to Shopping List or Delete Item

When you navigate away from the **Active** list, completed items that have not been deleted will show on the **Completed** list. Select "**Delete all**" from the completed list or delete them one at a time. You can also deselect the task (uncheck the box), and the task will return to the Active list.

On Echo Show: Say, "**Alexa, show my To-do list**," or "**what's on my To-do list**" and your Active list will appear:

- Swipe an item left to remove it
- To change something Alexa misheard, tap the item and use the back button to remove what's there and type in the correct task - not something we do often because this is more easily accomplished on the app on a computer
- Tap the item, tap the **X** and tap **Done** to remove it

If you say, "**Alexa, remove wash the car from my To-do list**," Alexa will give you verbal instructions on how to do it manually on the app.

Cards Created for List Items

A card is created on the app **Home** page when you add an item to the To-Do List. A box on the Card can be checked, and the item/task will be checked on the appropriate list in the app. The Card also offers the options we mentioned with each card such as "**Move item**" to the other list.

How we use the To-do List: We compile the list much like our shopping list - using all options. If one of us knows a handful of things that need doing, manually adding them on the app via the computer is easiest. Things that come to mind one at a time are more easily added by voice when at home and via the phone and app when away.

11. REMINDERS & ALARMS (& TIMERS)

We think you'll find these Alexa tools very useful, as we do - on nearly a daily basis.

When you select the **Reminders & Alarms** tab on the Alexa app, it opens to show a page with three options across the top: **Reminders, Alarms and Timers**.

The **Reminders** page is shown. Select either **Alarms** or **Timers** to use those functions. Let's review them individually.

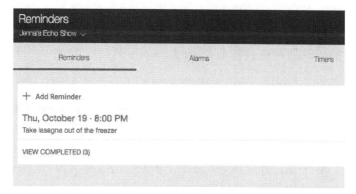

Reminders

How often do you forget something, even a minor task around the house, which is time sensitive? That's the key for us: We use Reminders when time is a factor. Otherwise, we add tasks to our To-do list. Sometimes we use both tools to be sure we do what we need to do and on time too!

Create Reminders: As with lists, you can set Reminders manually and using voice.

On the App: Typing in the Reminder ensures that the details are correct:

- Click or tap the blue + *Add Reminder*, and the Reminder form will appear.

- In the "*Remind me to...*" box, type in the specific reminder you want to hear, up to 128 characters.

- Select the *Date* tab, and today's date will appear in xx/yy/zzzz form. If the Reminder is for another day, select *Date* to change it. The month will be shaded blue. If that is correct, use the tab key or forward arrow key to move to day or year. Once you move on from the date, it will appear with the month spelled out.

- Select *Time*, and the current time will appear. Change it as you changed the date.

- Your device's name is shown. If you have more than one device on your Amazon account, select the down arrow to choose the device you want to give the Reminder.

- *Cancel* or *Save* the Reminder.

Using Voice: This is a much faster method of creating a Reminder. You can create Reminders using a specific time or asking for the Reminder to be made in a set amount of time:

- Say, "*Alexa, remind me to take lasagna out of the freezer at 8pm,*" or "*Remind me to leave for the show in 45 minutes.*"

- If you don't give a time, Alexa will ask you for one. Say, "*8pm,*" or "*in 45 minutes.*" When giving specific times and you forget the AM or PM, Alexa will ask, "Is that 8 this morning or evening?"

- If you give a specific time but no date, the Reminder will be set for today. To give a date, you can say things like "*today,*" or "*tomorrow.*" If you say, "*Friday,*" the Reminder will be set for the next Friday, and if you don't give a year, it will be set for the next time that date occurs. Of course, you can also give an exact time and date such as "*4pm on December 15.*"

- Alexa will affirm the reminder with, "OK, I'll remind you at 8pm" or "in 45 minutes."

Review and Manage Reminders:

- Manually select the ***Reminders & Alarms*** list to view your list of Reminders, or say, "***Alexa, show me my reminders,***" or "***What are my reminders?***"

- The list of Reminders will appear on the Show screen. Swipe any of them to the left to delete it. The Reminder will be removed from the App list too.

- You must manually edit a reminder; voice can't be used.

- Verbally cancel a Reminder by saying, "***Alexa, cancel the reminder for 8pm***," and Alexa will confirm the cancellation or ask a question to clarify. Here's a tip that applies anytime you converse with Alexa: When Alexa asks you a question and the light bar is blue/green, you don't have to use your wake word in your answer. The light bar indicates the device is listening.

- Choose **View Completed** at the bottom of the list to see past Reminders

- To **Edit** or **Mark as Completed**, select a Reminder from the list. Those two options will appear, and you can select your choice. When you select ***Edit***, the form will appear. Select what you want to change, make your edit, and select ***Save Changes***.

- To Delete the Reminder, select ***Edit*** and the ***Delete Reminder*** option

Getting Reminders: At the Reminder time, your Echo Show screen will display "***It's 8pm. Take lasagna out of the freezer.***" A chime will sound. This happens twice unless you select Dismiss from the screen. The screen will show the Reminder until you make another request or take an action using the Echo Show screen. This is quite helpful in cases where we're away from the Echo Show and don't hear the verbal reminder.

Completed Reminders: Reviewing them might help you remember whether you followed through on the action. Of course, the list only means that the Reminder was given, not that you took the lasagna out of the freezer! Adding the task to your To-do list and checking it off gives more assurance that it was done. For some reason Completed Reminders can't be deleted they just remain within the Completed page. To return to Active reminders from here, you must select the **Reminders & Alarms** tab from the menu of your Alexa app.

Alarms

The Alexa app has a few quirks, and one of them is that Alarms must be set verbally; there's no manual way to do it, probably because it's so easy using voice.

Creating an Alarm using Voice:

- Say, "**Alexa, set an alarm for 6:45am**." If you forget to specify any of the details, Alexa will ask.

- Alexa will affirm the alarm details, and the Echo Show screen will display the alarm. While the alarm is still on the screen, it can be swiped left to delete.

- You can also say, "**Alexa, set an alarm for 6:45am every morning**," or "**Set an alarm for 6:45am weekdays**," or "**weekends**," or even "**Set an alarm for 6.45am every Monday**."

- You can set multiple alarms for each day or different alarms for each day of the week.

- One-time alarms must be set for a time within the next 24 hours.

Managing Alarms: Alarms can be managed manually and with voice:

Using Voice:

- Say, "**Alexa, cancel the alarm for 6:45am**," whether it is a one-day or multi-day alarm. It will be turned off, and Alexa will affirm it. You cannot turn off a multi-day alarm for just one day. If you have a 6:45am weekday alarm, and you say, "**Alexa, cancel the 6:45am alarm for tomorrow**," Alexa will say, "you don't have an alarm set for tomorrow morning." Saying, "**Alexa, cancel the 6:45am alarm**" will turn it off for all days.

Using Voice and Echo Show:

- Say, "*Alexa, show my alarms,*" and alarms that are On will appear on the Echo Show screen.

- Slide any of them left to delete it. That's all that can be done using the touchscreen.

On the app: To see your Alarms, select the *Reminders & Alarms* tab and then *Alarms* from the three options at the top.

- Any alarm you've set, even if it has gone off or been cancelled, will appear in the list. You can toggle it on or off.

- To edit an alarm, select it from the list. Your editing options include time and frequency of alarm including options like Every Day, Weekends, Every Monday, etc. You can *Delete* the alarm there or select *Save Changes*, if it has been edited. If you don't make changes, select *Cancel* or simply click away.

- The current Alarm Sound will show. Select that box to see options for **Celebrity Voices** and for **Custom Sounds**. When you select one, a sample sound will be played on your computer or phone, but not on Echo Show. Celeb voices are fun, and Custom Sounds range from interesting (Rainier) to quirky (Adrift) to ethereal (Squared Waves) to very annoying (Countertop). We keep it fresh by mixing celeb voices in with standard sounds too.

Manage alarm volume and default sound: This option is shown above the list of alarms. Select it to:

- Review the alarm volume or drag it left (quieter) and right (louder) to adjust volume.

- Review and change the alarm sound.

The audio for notifications is discussed later. The **Request Sounds** option is quite straightforward. If you select *Start of Request*, a single tone will sound when you say the wake word to let you know Alexa is listening. Turning on *End of Request* will cause Alexa to sound a tone when the request is complete.

Timers

Timers are easy to set and come in quite handy for obvious uses like baking, but we also use them to be reminded it is time to leave for an appointment, a game on TV is about to start and many other one-time tasks. They're much like Reminders, but even easier to set.

Timers is the third option at the top of the **Reminders & Alarms** tab. They must be set with voice.

Setting Timers:

- Say, "*Alexa, set a timer for 20 minutes*" or any length of time from a second to 24 hours.
- Alexa will say, "*20 minutes starting now*," and the timer and countdown will display for a few seconds on Echo Show.
- During that initial display, the Timer can be swiped left to cancel.
- More than one Timer can be set, and they can be named, if that helps you keep them straight! Say, "*Alexa, set an oven timer for 90 minutes*" or "*Set a rice timer for 60 minutes*." This is invaluable when you're cooking a multi-course meal or when using timers for cooking and for other tasks too. Here's a tip: Using Reminders concurrently with Timers can be very helpful too. For example, when we know the dish in the oven needs 90 minutes, we set a timer. Then, we'll set Reminders such as, "*Alexa, remind me to start the rice in 30 minutes*" and "*Remind me to put the bread in to warm in an hour*."

Viewing and Managing Timers: Use voice, app and Echo Show screen to manage timers.

View timers on the app where they will be listed with a countdown in progress. Or ask Alexa something like, "*Alexa, show my Timers*," and they will display on the Echo Show screen. Whether you ask to see them, the Timer set to go off soonest will remain on the show screen, if you're not viewing other content.

- **Using voice:** Say, "*Alexa, cancel the 20-minute timer*," and Alexa will say, "20-minute timer cancelled."

- **Using the app:** Select a Timer from the list, and select the *Cancel* option. You can also select *Manage Timer Volume* to slide it left for quieter and right for louder. This volume does not change the general volume setting on the Echo Show.

- **Using Echo Show and voice:** Say, "*Alexa, show my timers*," and when they are displayed on the screen, swipe left on any you want to delete.

During the last ten seconds of a Timer, a counter will display on Echo Show. When the Timer sounds, the screen will show, "your 20 minute timer is done" and a Dismiss button will appear. Swipe up, in the direction of the arrow, to shut off the Timer.

Cancelled and completed Timers do not remain in the list as cancelled and completed Alarms do.

12. ROUTINES

A few words to Alexa can now put a series of customizable functions on auto-pilot, so to speak. The feature is called Routines, and here's how it works: You create a Routine once, select a request phrase or a time of day to trigger it, and the routine's functions occur without having to make separate requests for each one. Currently, though subject to change as all things with Alexa seem to be, Routines only works with:

- Smart Home automation devices
- Flash Briefing (News, sports, entertainment news, etc.)
- Weather information
- Traffic/Commute information

Each of these Alexa functions are discussed in other chapters, so reviewing them first will assist you in making the most of the possibilities available with Routines.

Still, its possibilities are limited. It would be helpful if a reading of your day's calendar schedule, playing the Tonight Show monologue from Skills (or starting any of the Skills you use), tuning to a specific radio station on Tunein or Playlist on Amazon Music were possible too, and we suspect features like that will be added to Routines.

Our first foray into Routines was an evening routine that goes like this:

- We say, "***Good evening,***" and...
- Alexa turns on automated interior and exterior lighting
- Echo Show plays our Flash Briefing to catch us up on the news of the day

We have a morning Routine too. At 7am, it starts our coffee pot, adjusts our smart thermostat a few degrees and plays our Flash Briefing, which starts with several sports briefings, and we often stop it after them because we peruse the news online while we have breakfast. A nighttime Routine that adjusted the thermostat and lights, locked doors and turned off the TV would be useful too, though we don't have enough home automation equipment to make it worthwhile yet.

Here's another "as of now" oddity we expect will change: There isn't a Routines tab on the Alexa app for PC; It can only be accessed on mobile apps.

OK, let's talk specifics on setting up Routines. We suggest that you go through this step-by-step with us because, frankly, the instructions make it sound more complicated than it is. You'll see how easy it is, if you follow along.

The first step is to choose Routines from the main Menu on your mobile device. From there:

- Tap the + *sign* at the top near Routines, and two options will show: **When this Happens** and **Add Action**
- The **When this Happens** is the trigger, and when you tap its + *sign*, you'll be given two options: **When you Say Something** and **At Scheduled Time**
- Selecting *When you Say Something* will open a keypad where you can type in the word or phrase to invoke the routine
- Select *At Scheduled Time*, and you'll see: *At Time* and *Repeat* options
- We tapped the at *Scheduled Time* option to select 7am on the clock dial that appears before selecting *OK* and *Done*
- Then we tapped the *Repeat* option to choose Weekdays from a list that also offered Weekends and individual days of the week

In true Amazon fashion, you can choose Weekdays, Weekends or ONE day of the week, but not two or more individual days of the week. Complete the trigger side of the equation by selecting Done.

Now you're finished with the trigger part - a word/phrase or time. The next step is to decide what happens. Select *Add Action*, and four options will appear: **News, Traffic, Weather** and **Smart Home**

- Choose the ones you want, one at a time, and follow the easy prompts to customize them before selecting **Add**

- Once you've set up the Routine, select **Create**, and it will be scheduled

Your Routines show in a list on the main Routines menu page. Select a routine to modify any of its options, delete it or toggle it Off (and later, back On, if desired).

As mentioned, setting up smart home skills, and traffic, news and weather briefings are discussed later in this guide so become familiar with these options before setting up any routines.

13. ALEXA SKILLS

With Skills, the potential to personalize your use of Alexa and the Echo Show is tremendous. An Alexa Skill, in simplest terms, is a third-party function that can be used with Alexa and the Echo Show - Find a recipe, order an Uber, ask quiz game questions, listen to the Tonight Show monologue, order pizza, find your phone, lead you through a short workout, turn on outdoor lighting... the spectrum is very diverse. Most Skills are easy to set up and use; There's a bit of a learning curve for a few of the more technical ones.

This guide will help you understand the basic concept of Skills, give tips for putting Alexa Skills to work for you and suggest a few to try.

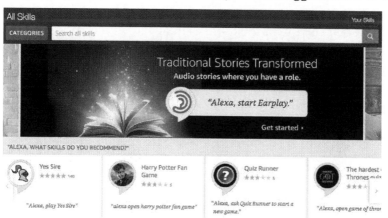

Let's go over the basic approach at the start to show that it's fairly easy:

- Find a Skill you want to use

- Enable the Skill by selecting the blue **Enable Skill** box (which will switch to **Disable Skill** when enabled)

- For some Skills, you will be asked to follow prompts to link an account or instructions for setting up the Skill for use, such as entering your phone number for a Find My Phone skill (Most of these types of Skills say **Account Linking Required** under the Enable button)

- Grant permissions (very few Skills require this) such as accessing your Echo Show device address to make the Skill more functional
- Once the Skill is active, ask Alexa to put the Skill to use, such as, *"Alexa use Find my Phone"* (There are "Say..." tips for every Skill)
- If the Skill is more than a one-time event like playing Jeopardy or listening to a radio station, control the Skill with voice requests such as *Pause, Resume* and *Stop*
- Disable a Skill by selecting it from the **Your Skills** list and choosing the *Disable* option
- (Optional) Rate the Skill and add your Review to assist others in picking useful Skills and avoiding duds

The list of Skills you have enabled is viewed by selecting the *Your Skills* tab at the top of the main Skills page on the app.

Deciding which Skill to try can be something of a challenge - harder than using most of them! There are more than 25,000 Skills divided into 21 categories. Many new Skills are added daily. Don't expect to browse them all - It's like walking into a bookstore and trying to read the front cover of every book on the shelves. That's unrealistic. Here's how we discover Skills:

- **Use the Search Box at the top:** This is always our first choice. It allows us to find exactly what we want or a Skill related to our interests. For example, one of us wants to brush up on the Spanish language skills learned in college, so the term *"Spanish lessons"* was typed into the box. Three Skills were displayed as results. We enabled two of them, tried them out, and disabled one.
- **Select the Categories Tab at the top:** Here, you can browse categories that interest you. We sometimes look at the New Arrivals category to try a few. When you select a Category, here's what you'll see:

1. The option to search within the Category: This saves a lot of time if you're looking for something specific.

2. The number of Skills in the Category

3. **Sort by:** The default Sort By method of listing Skills in each category is by Featured Skills. Select **_Sort By_** to change the listing to Relevance, Average Customer Rating or Release.

4. **Recommended for You:** We're never sure why the Skills in this list are recommended for you. Sometimes there seems to be a connection with other Skills we have Enabled. The arrow to the right of the list allows you to scroll and browse horizontally.

5. **Top Enabled Skills:** These are popular Skills with high ratings, usually 4.5 to 5 Stars. We rely heavily on the recommendations of others.

6. **A vertical list of the Skills in the Category:** These seem to be recently added Skills and Skills Amazon wants to feature.

- **Scan the Rows:** Each horizontal row has a different title, and rows can be browsed using the scroll arrow at right. Some of the many rows currently showing are titled:

1. **New Skills:** Newest "big name" Skills, currently Skills from Rosetta Stone, Nissan, Lexus

2. **Top Skills:** Skills that are highly rated and popular

3. **Recommended Skills:** Skills Amazon thinks fit you

4. **My Skills:** Your enabled Skills

5. **Game Skills:** Quizzes and similar games

6. **Morning Skills:** Starbucks Reorder, Daily Affirmation, Morning Music and similar

7. **Food and Drink Skills:** Recipes, Restaurants, Cooking Tips, etc.

Skills on Amazon.com: Skills can be searched, browsed and enabled at Amazon.com too. Hover over Departments, then hover down to Echo & Alexa. When you do, a topic list called **Content & Resources** will appear. Select *Alexa Skills* from the list. Or simply go here - **www.lyntons.com/AmSkills**

Tips for Picking Skills to Try and Managing Enabled Skills

These tips about deciding which Alexa Skills to try first should prove useful to you, as they have for us:

- **Read About This Skill and Skill Details:** When you select a Skill to consider it, read both these sections to learn what it does, how it does it and how the Skill is used. You'll have a clear idea whether the Skill is a good fit for you.

- **Go by Ratings and Reviews:** The average rating on Skills, as you can see, is about 3 Stars. We don't bother even trying Skills with fewer than 3 Stars. Many don't work well are simply aren't very useful. We much prefer 4-Star and above Skills. It's also helpful to open the Skill to read the reviews. Knowing why people like or dislike the Skill will help you decide if it will suit your purposes or not. This tip is very helpful when there are multiple Skills for many purposes like finding your phone (11 and growing) and finding a local restaurant (5).

- **Most Skills waste time:** It's easy to lose an hour or more browsing and trying Skills - and then wonder where the time went. Most Skills are not particularly useful. We're at the point where we only go looking for Skills if we have a specific purpose in mind like relearning Spanish. Sure, we have a few "fun" Skills enabled, but we find we use them less and less.

- **Disable Skills you don't like:** As soon as you realize a Skill doesn't work, wastes your time or in any other way isn't a good fit for you, disable it.

- **Disable Skills you don't use:** We go through our Skills once a month or so to weed out Skills we don't use. This unclutters our list and helps us find the Skill we do want at any given moment.

Develop a Skill to Share

Alexa Skills are developed by Fortune 500 companies and the guy living next door who does it for a hobby.

Anyone can develop a Skill and release it to be used, rated and reviewed. If that intrigues you, see the Amazon Developers Site that's all about creating Skills.

Check out **developer.amazon.com** and select **Alexa**. There, choose **Get Started with Alexa** to access what Amazon calls the Amazon Skills Kit, or ASK.

You have the option to use a Skills template or build one all your own. Developers are rewarded with perks from Amazon ranging from developer shirts to Echo devices.

14. SMART HOME

Smart home enthusiasts enjoy using Alexa because it allows them to control their smart home equipment with hands-free convenience. Wink, WeMo, Nest, ecobee, Phillips, SmartThings - Alexa integrates with most smart home equipment in five easy steps using Skills, the subject of the **last chapter**.

Setting Up Your Smart Home Devices

Here are the steps, all explained in detail below:

1. Verify that your smart home device works with Amazon Alexa by finding an Alexa Skill for it

2. Prepare the device for linking to Alexa

3. Enable the Alexa Skill for the device

4. Ask Alexa to discover the device, so it can be controlled using Alexa

Once you've setup your devices, and connected to Alexa, we will discuss how to get the most out of your smart home products by grouping them into Groups and Scenes.

Before we get into the details of these steps, it's always a good idea to put safety first. Amazon recommends:

- Use the smart home equipment only as recommended by the manufacturer, and follow its instructions
- Check to see that requests such as locking doors, closing the garage door and turning on security lighting have been carried out
- Once a device is connected to the Alexa app, it can be controlled by anyone who uses your Echo Show, so be sure to instruct

everyone in the household about the smart device's proper use

- Since home security is critical, consider turning off Echo device microphones to prevent unintended changes to locks, lighting and other security features

Let's work through these steps systematically giving step-by-step guidance where needed.

1. Verify Device Compatibility with Alexa

If it's compatible with Alexa, there will be a Skill for it:

- Select the **Skills** page within the Alexa app
- Type in the device name, such as WeMo, ISY or Samsung SmartThings
- Hit *Enter*
- Locate the device's Skill in the handful of results you get

Another option is to visit the Amazon Smart Home webpage and search that department for your smart home device. Devices compatible with Alexa will have a small "**Works with Amazon Alexa**" white banner on their product page. It's also worth visiting this department just to get a sense of what's available in the Smart Home marketplace right now. Visit - **www.lyntons.com/SmartHome**

2. Prepare the Device for Linking to Alexa

With the Skill located to verify compatibility, now it's time to get your smart home equipment ready. This is done independently and away from your Echo Show or Alexa app. Basically, you need to get any smart home device up and running correctly first before linking it with Alexa.

- Download the smart device app (available on the manufacturer's site) to a mobile device
- Use the device app to set up the smart home device on the same Wi-Fi network that Alexa is using (viewable on the Alexa app by going to *Settings > Your Echo > under Wireless*)

- Once the smart home device is online, download and install software updates if prompted

Note to Phillips Hue Bridge users: At this writing, the Hue Bridge works with Echo, Dot and Tap, but not Show. That might have changed by the time you read this, since the V2 (second generation Bridge) has been released. Check for a Skill or try pressing the Bridge button to see if it can be found by your Echo Show.

3. Enable the Alexa Skill for the Device

Now that your smart device is ready to go, enable its Skill, which you located in step 1 when verifying compatibility:

- Select the **Enable** box, and it will change to **Disable**, indicating the Skill has been enabled
- Read the information on the device's Skill page to discover the easiest and most effective way to use it with Echo Show including suggested voice commands
- When you later want to find the Skill, it will be in the Your Skills list which you get to from the Skills page of the Alexa app.

4. Ask Alexa to Discover the Device

There are two approaches:

- Say, "**Alexa discover devices**," and Alexa will search for them and report to you what was found
- Go to the **Smart Home** tab on the Alexa app, select **Devices**, and select the **Discover** box there
- **Note:** The Enabled Skills for your smart home device should also be listed on the Smart Home page on the app

Getting the Most Out of your Smart Home Devices

You should now have all your smart home devices connected to Alexa and be able to see them all within the Smart Home page of your Alexa app. So now let's look at bundling them together by placing them in

Groups and/or managing Scenes to get the most functionality from your automated household

Organize Smart Home Groups:

Putting devices into a Group allows you to turn multiple devices on or off with a single voice command.

Here's how to create and manage a group:

- Select the **Smart Home** tab from the Menu
- Select **Groups** and then **Add Group.** You will be given two options, you should select **Smart Home Group**. If you have multiple Echo devices then you can learn more about the other option here (**Multi-Room Music Group**) in our **Help & Feedback chapter**.
- Create a name for the group that is at least two syllables, distinct from other group names and spelled properly. Alternatively, select one of the common group names that Alexa offers.
- Pick which devices you want in the group
- Select **Save**
- Try controlling the group with a single command such as "**Alexa, turn on Living Room**," or "**Alexa, lock doors**."
- Edit a Group using the Add/Remove devices option in the Groups section of the Smart Home page, or select Delete Group to eliminate it

Create and Manage Scenes:

With Groups you are simply putting different devices together so you can switch them all on and off at once. Scenes are a little more sophisticated and harder to quantify in this guide because they are specific to the smart home devices that you own.

So a Scene is an action/feature that you have set up separately within the manufacturer's app of your smart home devices. When you connect that device to Alexa any Scene that you previously setup should now appear in the Alexa app when you navigate to **Smart Home > Scenes**

To manage all the available Scenes select the Scenes tab on the Smart Home page in the Alexa app

- Follow the prompts to customize the Scene produced by your smart devices
- Select the Scene to edit or delete it

See Skill page of each device for suggestions about controlling it using voice. Most are straightforward and predictable. For example, say: "**Alexa...**"

- *Turn on or off a smart home device, group or scene"*
- *Brighten or dim a single light or group"*
- *Set the light to pink/soft white"*
- *Set the thermostat to 70 degrees"*
- *Lock the back door or lock the doors"*

Troubleshooting Smart Home Setup

Try these Alexa smart home tips in this order, starting with the most likely problems:

- Double-check compatibility of the smart home device with Alexa
- Make sure the device's Skill is enabled
- Download the latest device software update

- Restart Wi-Fi, your Echo Show devices and the smart home device(s)

- Disable and Enable the Skill

- Unlink the smart device from Alexa using the *"Forget"* option for the device

- Follow the setup steps above to relink Alexa and the device

Troubleshooting Wi-Fi Issues with Smart Home equipment:

The most common problem is that the Echo Show and the smart home devices are not on the same Wi-Fi network. If you want to change the network the Show is on:

- Go to *Echo Show Settings*, by sliding down on the screen, starting above the display, and choosing *Settings* from the Menu

- Check the Wi-Fi network that the Echo Show is on - it's listed under the **Wi-Fi** tab

- If the Echo Show is not on the network the smart devices are on, tap the *Wi-Fi* option, tap the correct network and type in its password before tapping *Done*

- Optionally, and if this is something in your technological skill set, tap the *Add a Network* option in the *Wi-Fi Settings*, and add a network for Echo Show and the smart home devices (for preventing interference from other devices on the network)

Try to Discover Devices Again: After making any necessary changes outlined above, ask Alexa to *"discover devices"* again. If the reply is "I didn't find any devices" or the device in question wasn't discovered, contact the smart home device's manufacturer. After all, it is up to the device manufacturer to ensure its equipment is compatible with Alexa.

Top Smart Home Alexa Skills

There are about 700 Skills in the Smart Home category, and like Skills in all categories, some are more useful than others. Here are some Skills that work as advertised and offer genuine benefit, in our opinion:

ICMYCloud (4 Stars): Allows you to watch your home's CCTV surveillance cameras on Echo Show. Say, for example, *"**Alexa show my front door camera**"* or *"**Show my pool camera**"* to monitor your home's security.

Ecovacs Deebot (3.5 Stars): Allows you to control most Deebot vacuum models using Alexa. Say, *"**Alexa ask Deebot to start cleaning**"* or *"**Ask Deebot to start charging.**"*

Kenmore Smart (3.5 Stars): Allows you to monitor and control some Kenmore Smart and Elite home appliances. Say, *"**Alexa ask Kenmore Smart what is my freezer temperature**"* or *"**Ask Kenmore Smart to start the dryer.**"*

ADT Smart Security (4 Stars): Allows you to monitor and control your ADT home security system. Say, *"**Alexa ask Smart Security to run 'daytime'**"* or *"**Alexa, ask Smart Security to run 'dinner party.'**"*

To find Skills for your smart home equipment, search for your equipment brand in the Smart Home Skills category. Give the Skills a try. If they're useful, you've added convenience and functionality to your life. If not, disable them and try something else. That's how we do it, and it allows us to find Skills we use rather than those that clutter our Skills list waiting to be disabled.

15. THINGS TO TRY

You won't use Alexa and Echo Show long before you realize Amazon is constantly suggesting something for you to try.

That's what this chapter is about...

Most of the topics in the **Things to Try** section of the app are clear and straightforward.

Our goal in this chapter is to uncover things that aren't as clear and give you inside tips from experienced

Alexa users that should assist you in getting the most from your Echo Show.

The Things to Try section is just a list. When you select any of the topics, you're taken to another part of the app, usually **Help & Feedback** or **Settings**.

The reason to discuss any of it here rather than wait until the next two chapters is that this list covers the most useful topics, at least in the minds of the folks at Amazon.

We'll cover Help & Feedback and Settings next while trying not to get bogged down in the redundancy built into the app. In short, we'll cover everything before we're done.

By the way, topics are frequently added and removed from this list, so our discussion that follows might not include all the topics you currently see on the list.

Sign up to our newsletter to stay abreast of developments and changes - **www.lyntons.com/updates**

Our Approach to Things to Try

We'll list each category in the Things to Try section, give a brief overview and then share tips for getting the most from that Thing to Try. Here we go!

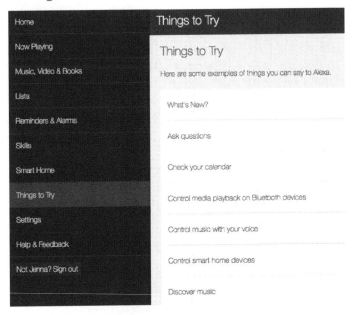

What's New

This is a random and changing assortment of new features and things to try, though Amazon keeps some topics here longer than others. Some What's New topics are explained here.

For others, you're invited to ask Alexa about the topics with suggestions like, "*Alexa, Tell me about the all-new Echo/Echo Plus/Echo Spot.*" Links are included with some topics, usually to other sections on the Things to Try app - and we'll cover those topics as we work through this chapter.

Tips: This section can be a rabbit hole of information, not all of it useful but certainly time-consuming. We suggest scanning it occasionally, trying a few things that look useful, interesting or fun, and, unless you have a lot of time on your hands, leaving the rest alone.

Echo Show

This section is all about what Amazon's latest Echo device can do for you, especially things that other Echo devices cannot do like show movie trailers (discussed earlier) and show your Prime Photos, discussed later.

Tips: Alexa and the Echo Show gain new capabilities consistently. Reviewing this section for things you didn't know they could do will keep you up to speed and getting maximum value from your investment.

Ask Questions

This topic is aptly named - a list of questions in a spectrum of categories to ask Alexa.

Tips: We're still amazed at how quickly Alexa taps information sources for a wide range of knowledge like the Pittsburgh Pirates won the 1960 World Series and the distance to Jupiter is 391,000,000 miles. We most often ask how to spell words (well, one of us does), math questions (the other one does that) and general knowledge questions. If you ask a general knowledge question, remember your query will produce a Card viewable on the **Home** page with a link to a Wikipedia article on the subject.

Ask for Recipes

Amazon has partnered with All Recipes and suggests a range of questions regarding quick recipes, common favorites and what can be made with the items you have on hand.

When you ask a question, a horizontal list, complete with tantalizing pictures, appears on Echo Show, and Alexa reads off the entries. Tap an entry to see an ingredients list. Tap the ***Directions*** option for a step-by-step guide to a perfect dish.

Tips: We tried the All Recipes Skill, now hovering at about 2 Stars. We didn't like it either. Using Ask Alexa (without the need to Enable the All Recipes Skill) is fast and easy. We have the most fun asking Alexa what can be made with a few things we have on hand like, *"Alexa, find me a recipe using chicken, black beans, vegan sausage and noodles,"* for example. Then, we browse the recipes and ingredients list before voting on our choice to try. The recipes in the list are rated with 1-5 Stars along with the number of ratings. Preparation and cooking time and number of servings are listed too

Calling and Voice Messaging

This is one of the newest features on Echo devices, Echo-to-Echo, hands-free communication. It's sure to grow with time. We cover this topic in the **Help & Feedback Chapter**.

Tips: Read our section on it, first. Then, implement it cautiously. Giving people one more way to get in touch with you can be helpful in some cases and annoying in others. Thankfully, Echo Show's Calling feature can be turned off to protect your "quiet time," and turned back on just as easily.

Check Your Calendar

Alexa can link to calendars from Google, Apple and Microsoft. Then, you can ask Alexa questions like, *"Alexa, how does my day look?"* Alexa will remind you of your appointments. This feature is discussed in the **Settings Chapter**.

Tips: Couples have the option of having two calendars and linking them, a slightly more complex and hard-to-check setup, or using just one calendar. It really depends on how busy each of you are. We tried both, and that helped us decide which one works best for us, given our circumstances.

Connect Bluetooth Devices

This is a topic covered in **Chapter 2** and again later in **Help & Feedback** which will be useful if you want to listen to music from your phone or tablet.

Tips: Make sure Bluetooth is turned on in your device's **Settings**. You'll see the Echo Show listed as **Echo Show—***** (where *** is three random letters and numbers) in the list of pairable options.

Control Music

We covered this topic in the **Music Chapter**, but reading the list on this page of the app might give you an idea or two we missed or you forgot.

Tips: If you have more than one Echo device, you will definitely want to explore the Multi-Room Music section covered in the **Settings Chapter**.

Control Smart Home Devices

Mostly just a list of things to say, the page does have a useful link at the bottom where you can learn more about **Supported Smart Home Devices** for Alexa.

Tips: Patience is a virtue! Some devices sync easily; it seems impossible to link others. Review **Chapter 14** on Smart Home, and follow the steps carefully. If they don't work for your device, and you're sure it is compatible, contact the device manufacturer.

Control the Color of Smart Lights

More than 40 smart bulbs now work with Alexa and Echo Show. Once lighting and Alexa are linked, smart lights provide functionality and customizable ambience you'll enjoy.

Tips: See our tips from the previous section. They apply here too.

Discover Music

Explore what is available in your music options such as Music Library, Prime Music, Spotify and iHeartRadio by asking Alexa questions related to your favorite artists.

Tips: If you don't have an artist in mind, ask, *"Alexa, what's new in music?"* and Alexa will display 50 songs on Echo Show that can be scrolled horizontally and tapped to play or learn more.

Drop In - Alexa's Intercom System

Echo devices can be used like intercoms, a topic covered in our section on Calling and Messaging (**Chapter 15**).

Tips: There are privacy concerns with Drop In, so read up on the details we provide, and proceed with caution.

Enable Skills

Skills are things you can do with Alexa and Echo Show with a third-party app, called a Skill.

Tips: Chapter 13 is all about Alexa Skills including plenty of step-by-step guidance. See especially our Tips for Picking Skills to Try and Managing Enabled Skills.

Find Local Businesses and Restaurants

Ask Alexa what restaurants, auto repair shops, clothing stores, dentists, etc., are nearby, and an Alexa-narrated list will display on Echo Show.

The list can be scrolled, and businesses can be tapped for more details including phone numbers. We cover this in more depth in **Chapter 15**, Things to Try.

Tips: Set your device location/address in *Settings* under the name of your Echo Show. Choose the *Edit* option, and type in your street (52nd Street), your block (3700 52nd Street) or your complete address (3749 52nd Street). The more exact you are, the more closely the results will be to your location, especially the distance given to each of the businesses.

Find Traffic Information

Alexa will give you the fastest route for your commute or trip and how long it is expected to take. The topic is covered in **Chapter 15.**

Tips: Before you're rushed to get out the door to work or another destination, go to *Settings* and *Traffic* to enter *From* and *To* locations, so all you have to do is ask, *"Alexa, how long is my commute?"*

Fun and Games

This is a list of silly things to interact with Alexa about - Jokes, Alexa's talents, games and more. There's also a link to the Games and Trivia section of Skills.

Tips: Get ready to groan when listening to Alexa's jokes, limericks and puns! They're fun and family friendly although Alexa's unemotional voice doesn't help comic delivery!

Get Weather Updates

Alexa will give you a weather report based on your location, or you can ask for the temperature or weather in another location. Ask any weather question, and you'll see a 7-day forecast on Echo Show.

Tips: For greatest accuracy, edit your *Location* under *Settings* and *your Echo Show*.

Go to the Movies

Alexa narrates a list of movies playing near you as their "posters" appear on Echo Show. The list can be scrolled left. Tap a movie for details on story and actors. Tap *Watch Trailer* to see it on Echo Show. Tap *Showtimes* for details.

Tips: As with many of these Things to Try, giving your location in *Settings* will provide results for movies nearest you.

Hear the News

Your news on the Echo Show comes in the form of a Flash Briefing. Most news and entertainment organizations produce regular (hourly/daily/weekly) summaries of local/national/world news or news about their industry. Some are video. In the *Flash Briefing* section of the *Settings*, you can browse hundreds of content providers. They can be selected one at a time to be added to your Flash Briefing. The order can be edited. Then, when you ask for your Flash Briefing, your news summaries play in the order you've selected.

Tips: Start with content from sources you know and trust, and then expand outward to new sources that sound important, interesting or otherwise appealing. We have an eclectic mix of about 30 sources. The most important to us, about 7, are first in line, and the rest follow. With that arrangement, we get the news we want to hear most when time is limited, and we can hear/watch the entire Briefing while we're relaxing on the deck or doing housework.

Keep Up With Your Sports Teams

In *Settings > Sports Update*, you can search for your favorite teams to add to the list. When you ask for your Sports Update, like a Flash Briefing, you hear the latest scores and upcoming games. Impressively, you can also ask questions about the statistics of any player.

Tips: The Sports Update section lists professional leagues in North America and Europe you can select from. But don't overlook the fact that most college teams are available for your Sports Update too. Just search them.

Listen to Audible Audiobooks

We've covered Audible in detail in **Chapter 9** on Books. This is a service we think is worth trying.

Tips: Try syncing all your connected devices, so you can listen to a book on any of them. Start at home, switch to your phone later, for example, and the book will pick up right where you left off.

Listen to Amazon Music

This feature was thoroughly discussed in the **Music Chapter**. Amazon Music refers to one of the music subscriptions available from Amazon.

About 2 million songs are offered on Prime Music; Music Unlimited has closer to 30 million.

Tips: Try Amazon Prime, not just for the 2 million songs, but many other perks which can be viewed on the Try Prime tab on most pages of Amazon.com.

Listen to Kindle Books

Kindle fans will enjoy this feature, though this is listening rather than reading. While Audible books are read by the author or a performer, Kindle books are read by Alexa.

Tips: Certain perks of Kindle Unlimited are part of an Amazon Prime membership. We're not on Amazon's payroll, we just get a lot of value from our Prime membership.

Listen to Podcasts and Radio

This refers to Tunein and iHeartRadio, both covered in the **Music Chapter**. Both services offer a range of streaming live radio options and archived podcasts.

Tip: Both services have free accounts and premium accounts. We started with a free account and upgraded to a paid option on one of the services. Listening to music, a podcast or a game is so easy with Echo Show's hands-free functionality.

Shopping

An Amazon device must feature a shopping option, right? Ask Alexa to shop for an item you want, and options will appear on Echo Show to browse, learn more about and purchase, of course.

Tips: If you turn on the Purchase by Voice option in Settings and Voice Purchasing, turn on the Voice Code option and add a code. This will prevent accidental ordering of stuff you were just browsing.

Set Alarms/Set Reminders/Set Timers

These three sections are very similar, easy to use and have many uses. We covered each in detail in **Chapter 11** where they can be reviewed.

Tips: Review what we said about using Reminders and Timers concurrently when making a large meal. We also use a combination of them during busy days at home when it's easy to forget to tackle tasks we need to complete.

To-Do's and Shopping Lists

Creating and managing To-do and Shopping Lists with voice, the Alexa app and the Echo Show is easy, and the lists are tools you'll use daily, if you're like us. See our **Chapter on Lists** for full details about To-do and Shopping lists.

Tips: Learn all three options - voice, the app and your Echo Show to create and manage your lists, because there are times, for example, using voice might disturb someone that is sleeping, while at other times, voice is much more convenient than manually interacting with the app or Echo Show. Also, download the Alexa app to your mobile device. Having both lists, not just your shopping list, with you when out and about will be prove helpful.

Use These Phrases Anytime

This list of basic phrases is a good reminder of all the things Alexa and the Echo Show can do.

Tips: Try some of the suggestions on this list to get more from your device.

More Alexa Products to Try

There's more here than just links to Echo devices. The link to Alexa-enabled products takes you to Amazon where you can browse thermostats, lighting, phones, watches, Bluetooth speakers and many more items that offer built-in Alexa functionality.

Tips: Before you buy an Alexa-enabled device, read lots of reviews, including good and bad, to get a full picture of what the device can and cannot do, its reliability, how hard it is to set up and get connected to Alexa, etc.

16. SETTINGS

Settings is where you turn on or off features and modify others to suit your preferences. In short, Alexa Settings allow you to customize the app and Echo Show. Let's look together at the **Settings** page on the Alexa app where we will take the topics from top to bottom (we recommend doing this on a pc or mac at **alexa.amazon.com**.

Note that some Settings are available via the Echo Show screen. Swipe down to reveal the Show's Menu, and tap *Settings* to see what's there. Where applicable, we'll discuss the device Settings too.

Devices

Do Not Disturb	
Do Not Disturb	On
Scheduled Off	>
General	
Sounds	>
Device name	Jenna's Echo Show Edit
Device location The location will be used for weather and other local features.	

This section lists by name the devices and apps connected to this Amazon.com account and to the accounts of others in your Amazon Household. An option to **Set Up a New Device** is given too. When you set up a device, you give it a name. When you download the app to a mobile device or use it online at **alexa.amazon.com**, the apps are named after the device. Whether the device is Online or Offline is shown beneath its name.

Echo Show Settings

Select your Echo Show from the device list, and let's explore what's there.

- **Do Not Disturb:** Turn this on to stop Calls, Messages, Drop-ins and Notifications. It does not prevent you from interacting with Echo Show and using music services, shopping and other features. Do Not Disturb remains On until you turn it Off.

- **Scheduled Off:** If you have a regular time during the day when you want Echo Show to be quiet unless you make a request:

  1. Choose **Scheduled Off**

  2. Turn on Scheduled by selecting the **On/Off** box, which will turn blue for On

  3. Choose **Edit**

  4. Click or tap the Hour, Minute and AM/PM boxes one at a time, and make your selection for **Daily Start Hour** and **End Hour**

  5. Select **Save Changes** to make the change or select **Cancel** to keep the schedule as it is

- **Do Not Disturb on Echo Show:** Slide down on the screen to show the Menu. Tap the **Do Not Disturb** symbol to turn the feature On or Off. You can also turn it On/Off and adjust the time of Scheduled On by going to **Settings on** the screen. Scroll down and tap Do Not Disturb

  1. Turn the feature on by tapping the **On/Off** oval

  2. Tap **Scheduled** and tap the **Oval** to turn it on

  3. Tap **Starts** to set or change the start time

  4. Tap the **Hour** and **Minute**, and use the clock face to set the time

  5. Tap **AM** or **PM** to complete setting a Start Time

  6. Tap **Ends** to set or change the end time in the same manner

- **Do Not Disturb with Voice:** Say, "**Alexa do not disturb,**" a chime will sound, Alexa will confirm your request and the screen will darken. The Do Not Disturb icon will be lit in Echo Show Settings. Say, "*Alexa, turn off do not disturb,*" to reverse these actions.

General Settings

- **Sounds:** This is where you choose the volume and what sounds you hear from Echo Show.

  1. **Alarm, Timer and Notification Volume:** Click or tap the volume bar, and drag it left for quieter and right for louder. This bar does not change the general volume on the Echo Show. That can be done by saying, "*Alexa, volume 7,*" or using the - and + buttons on top of the Echo Show.

  2. **Notifications Sound:** Turn on the box to play a sound when notifications (such as your Amazon order has shipped) or messages (sent by your contacts) arrive. Notifications are explained in **Chapter 17**.

  3. **Custom Sounds - Alarm:** Currently, custom sounds are available only for the Alarm. Your current sound will be shown; select the box to change the sound. The Alarm sound is discussed in detail in **Chapter 11** on Reminders & Alarms.

  4. **Request Sounds - Start/End of Request:** If you turn these boxes On, you will hear a sound as soon as Alexa starts listening and when Alexa has stopped listening and is processing your request. Give it a try. We and most of those we've surveyed about it have turned these sounds off.

  5. All these Sounds Settings can be managed on Echo Show too. Slide down on the screen, and tap *Settings* in the Menu. Tap *Sounds*, and make your adjustments or tap a subcategory such as *Alarm* or *Notification* to customize the sounds you hear.

- **Device Name:** This is the name you gave your Echo Show at set up. Choose the *Edit* option to change its name.

- **Device Location:** If you haven't set a location, you will see No Zip Code Set with the option to edit that and add a street address. The more specific you make the address, the more accurate the information you'll receive when asking about weather, restaurants, businesses, movie theaters and other nearby locations.

- **Device Time Zone:** Find your country or region in the top *Select a Region* box and your time zone in the *Select a Time Zone* box to get accurate time information.

- **Wake Word:** The default wake word is Alexa. Select the box to change it to Amazon, Echo or Computer and choose *Save*. As we've noted, we tried others and found that Amazon and Computer come up too often in our non-Alexa discussions to use because Alexa wakes but doesn't understand what we're talking about. Echo is a good option, if you don't like using Alexa.

  1. The Wake Word can also be changed on the Echo Show screen. Select *Settings*, scroll to *Device Options* and Select *Wake Word*. Tap your preference.

- **Measurement Units:** Change the measuring units to metric by selecting the boxes, or keep/turn them off for imperial units (Fahrenheit, yards, feet, inches, etc.).

  1. These units can be changed on the Echo Show too. In Settings, select *Device Options*. Temperature and Distance are two separate Settings. Choose either one, and tap your preference.

- **About:** The only Setting of importance here is the Reset to Factory Settings box. If you choose it, your History and Settings modifications will be lost. We suggest only doing this if you sell/ give your Echo Show or if you've set up the Show on the wrong Amazon account by accident.

  1. You can also do this on Echo Show by selecting *Settings* and *Device Options*. Tap *Reset to Factory Defaults* and confirm or cancel your choice.

Accounts

Settings

Devices

Jenna's Echo Show
Online

Set up a new device

Accounts

Notifications

Music & Media

Flash Briefing

Sports Update

Traffic

This section is more of a miscellaneous category. Most of the Settings don't require an outside account. We've discussed some of these already. Others we will put off until the next chapter on **Help & Feedback.**

- **Notifications:** There is currently only one notification type here, a ***Shipment Notification***. Select it, read the description, and turn on the box if you want to receive a notification on Echo Show to make you aware a shipment is expected.

- **Music & Media:** These tabs have been covered in the **Music Chapter,** but here is a brief review. Click any of the Music Service tabs for options such as ***Link/Unlink your Account*** and Go to the service's website. The ***Choose Default Music Service*** box at the bottom of the list allows you to choose the Music Library (Amazon Music or Spotify) and the Station Service (Amazon Music, Pandora and iHeartRadio) from where

Alexa will get the music you request unless you specify another service in your request. Click or tap your preferences, and choose **Done**.

- **Flash Briefing:** A Flash Briefing is news and information in the form of summaries from hundreds of sources now creating them. This section of Settings allows you to create, review and manage your personalized Flash Briefing:

    1. The main page shows your current Flash Briefing content providers, whether they are turned On or Off and the order of those turned On.

    2. Select the **Get More Flash Briefing Content** option to see all the sources. Rows are categorized by content and can be scrolled horizontally, and you can scroll down too.

    3. Once there, another option is to use the Search box to locate specific providers such as a TV/Radio station or network, newspaper, magazine or organization or to see what comes up when you search a genre like entertainment, sports, medicine or politics.

    4. Most of the sources are Alexa Skills. Review each Skill page for details, or simply Enable the Skill for each source you want as part of your Flash Briefing.

    5. As you compile a list of Flash Briefing sources, they appear on the main **Settings > Flash Briefing** page in the On section with their On/Off boxes blue for On. Select the box to turn any of them Off, and they will move to the lower Off section.

    6. Select Edit Order, and the list will be shown with three horizontal lines next to each source. Click or tap and hold the lines for any of them, and drag it up or down in the order.

    7. To listen, say, "**Alexa, play Flash Briefing**" or simply "**Alexa, Flash Briefing**", and it will begin on Echo Show in your preferred order.

8. You can control what you hear by saying, *"Alexa...Skip, Next, Go back"* or by tapping the Echo Show screen and tapping the forward or back arrow. You can also say *"Pause"* and *"Resume,"* or tap the screen to use the Pause/Play button.

- **Sports Update:** This feature is like the Flash Briefing accept that the news is delivered by Alexa:

  1. Compile the list of teams you want to follow using the Search box. The list of current North American and European professional sports leagues you can select teams from is found on the Things to Try page by selecting *Keep Up with Your Sports Teams*.

  2. College teams aren't listed, but they can be searched. For example, typing Texas into the search box produces a list of results that includes Texas A&M Aggies Basketball and Texas A&M Aggies Football as separate options along with options for five other colleges.

  3. Select any team, and it will appear on the main **Sports Update** page in a list showing the team and sport.

  4. Delete any of them using the *X*.

  5. You can't drag the teams up or down to change their order. The only option is to delete them and then add them again in the order you want to hear them.

  6. Say, *"Alexa, Sports Update"* to hear it. Updates are given only for teams that are currently in their season.

  7. While the update is playing, control what you hear by saying, *"Skip"*, *"Next,"* *"Go back"* or by tapping the Echo Show screen and tapping the forward or back arrow. You can say *"Pause"* and *"Resume,"* or tap the screen to use the Pause/Play button.

- **Traffic:** Find out how long your trip will take if you leave now. The Traffic form shows your "From" location as the location you've entered in Settings for your device location: **Settings > Devices > Your device > Device Location**. Choose **Edit** to change the address. If you give your complete address rather than just your Zip Code or street, your traffic commute time will be more accurate. Select **Settings > Traffic** to:

1. View your From location, and select **Change Address** if necessary to edit the location

2. Add a To location or change it with the **Change Address** option. We suggest entering the place you go the most as the To location - your workplace, school, parent's or children's home, for example. Change it anytime.

3. Choose the **Add Stop** option to include a location where you plan to stop along the way. This can later be deleted or changed using the options shown.

4. Alexa responds to "**Alexa, Traffic update**," "**My commute**," "**How's traffic**" and similar requests.

5. While Alexa is giving you the update, the drive time is shown along with one or more alternate routes.

- **Calendar:** Alexa works with Google, Microsoft and Apple calendars. Ask Alexa to add an event to your calendar on a day and time, and it will be done. Alexa will confirm, and your calendar for the next two days will appear on Echo Show. Here's how to set up and use a calendar with Alexa:

1. Choose the calendar you want to link.

2. Select the **Link your Calendar Account**, and a window will open on the service you've chosen, such as Google.

3. Sign into the account. You might have to enter a username, email or phone plus your password.

4. You'll be asked to give Alexa permission to have access to your calendar and possibly other information. For Microsoft,

Alexa also wants to Read your Profile, Read your Contacts and Access your Info Anytime

5. Select **Yes** to link the account or **No** to cancel the link.

6. Links are shown on the main Calendars page in Settings next to each service. For example, our page says 1 Linked Account next to Microsoft and Google.

7. Below the list, you can select the default Calendar from the list. Select the box, and your linked accounts will appear. Choose your preferred Calendar.

8. Start adding items to your Calendar using voice. If you leave out a detail such as the day/date or time, Alexa will ask.

9. Each added Calendar event is confirmed by Alexa verbally and by displaying the item, date and time on Echo Show.

10. To view or manage your Calendar on Echo Show, say, "*Alexa, show my Calendar*" to see the Calendar or "*What's on my Calendar?*" to both see and hear what's there. In this option, Alexa will announce your next scheduled event. To delete an event, tap the screen and tap the **Delete** button and then confirm delete.

11. Once you've asked for your Calendar, it will remain on the screen for about a minute if no other requests are made involving the Echo Show screen.

12. **Note:** You **will NOT receive reminders** on Echo Show when an event time arrives. That's why we use Reminders in addition to putting things on the calendar. For example, if we want to be somewhere at 7pm that's a 30-minute drive, we'll set a Reminder - something like "*Alexa, remind me at 6:15pm today that it's almost time to leave.*"

13. **Note:** If one of your calendars is linked, anyone can say, *"Alexa, what's on my Calendar"* to hear it.

14. Select any linked Calendar from the app to manage its Settings such as Show Holidays in the United States

15. The Calendar's setting page also has an option to ***Unlink this Calendar Account***. Selecting that option unlinks the account with no confirmation or further action required. The Link your Calendar Account appears again for future use.

- **Lists:** You have To-do and Shopping Lists with Alexa. You can link those lists to list services Any.do, AnyList and Todoist and others that have produced Skills. When you Enable one of these, your Alexa To-do and Shopping Lists will sync with the Skill, and you can use the Skill to read or add items, depending on how you manage the Settings. Your options are available under ***Settings > Lists***.

   1. Select any of the list Skills to view information about the Skill such as a summary of how it works, its rating and individual user reviews.

   2. Select the blue ***Enable*** button to try the Skill

   3. Link your Alexa lists to the Skill service by following the prompts that include giving the Skill provider permission to Read your Alexa Lists and to Write new items onto either list. These permissions can be changed by selecting the ***Settings*** tab on the Skill. This is also where you can ***Unlink*** the accounts.

   4. Once connected, you can go to the Skill provider, Any.do for example, to Read or Add items to an Alexa list based on the permissions you've given.

   5. **Our suggestion:** When it comes to this sort of thing, our motto is "just because it can be done doesn't mean it should be done." If you already use one of these handy list services, then linking the account to Alexa might serve a useful purpose. We

find that with the Alexa app on our computers and mobile devices and available for the asking on Echo Show, no other list service is needed. The added convenience of Alexa Reminders makes additional lists unnecessary for us.

- **Voice Purchasing:** To make shopping on Amazon fully hands-free, turn on Voice Purchasing:

  1. Go to **Settings > Voice Purchasing**

  2. Turn on **Purchase by Voice** by selecting the On/Off box - it will turn blue

  3. Select **View Payment Settings** to be taken to Amazon. com to ensure you have a valid 1-click payment method on file. The link will open in a new window where you will see Payment Settings with your Default 1-Click Payment Method. Select **Edit Payment Method** to be taken to your payment page on Amazon to manage your payment options.

  4. **Strongly Advised:** Use the 4-digit Voice Code option to eliminate accidental ordering or unauthorized purchases.

  5. Your next option is to allow "recognized" speakers to order without the code. Alexa creates what it calls a Voice Profile for each person using its impressive voice recognition technology. If you keep this option Off, as we do, the code will be required for every purchase. If you turn it On, then "recognized speakers" won't have to use a code.

- **In an Amazon Household With:** An Amazon Household is a group of Amazonians that share one another's music, books, payment methods and more. Households must contain at least 1 and up to 2 adults, up to 2 teens and up to 4 pre-teens. We talked about creating an Amazon Household in the **Chapter on Music**, and full details are available on Amazon.com. Select the **Accounts & Lists** tab rather than just hovering over it. When the page opens, select **Amazon Household** in the **Shopping Programs and Rentals** box. Alternatively follow this link: **www.amazon.com/myh/manage**. We've created a Household and enjoy it mostly for sharing music, books and other content.

General

The only Setting of importance here is **History**. Every time you speak to Alexa, a recording is made. Note that this list overlaps with the Cards viewable on the app Home page but is not identical. Not all voice interaction with Alexa produces a Card. We don't pay any attention to this, but here's how to manage this History:

- Select any entry to review its details
- Answer whether Alexa heard you properly
- Delete the voice recording
- Note that deleting a voice recording also deletes the Card, but it doesn't work conversely. If you choose Delete on a Card, the voice recording remains as part of Alexa's efforts to understand your voice profile more accurately.

To delete all voice recordings at once, you must deregister your Echo Show, also termed *Reset to Factory Defaults*. You should deregister/reset your device when getting rid of it.

17. HELP & FEEDBACK

Help & Feedback is the most comprehensive page/section of the app. Many of its topics are listed in **Chapter 15** - Things to Try and explained there.

At the top of the main Help & Feedback page is a list of User Guides for Alexa and Echo devices. We'll cover the Alexa and Echo Show. Most topics here are explained clearly in the app, so we won't waste your time with rehashing them. These topics may change as Amazon updates the Alexa app.

The Alexa App User Guide

Select Alexa to open the Guide to browse topics of interest or to find helpful information to make using Alexa easier and more functional.

Alexa Device Support

- **Accessibility Features:** Accessibility functions are built into Alexa, and the app is usable with Vision and Hearing equipment you might already have such as the screen readers listed. Echo Show has a screen reading function - covered shortly.

- **About Amazon Alexa:** This is an overview of Alexa/Echo Show capabilities. While we've covered most topics, if you're still unclear about anything, a wealth of details is here. Let's hit one not covered elsewhere:

Calling and Messaging

Alexa has impressive device-to-device communication skills. Patience in setting them up and learning how to use them will be rewarded. It's not hard, just a multi-step task that is fully detailed in the Alexa app under this heading.

Alexa-to-Alexa Calls: This feature allows you to call another Alexa user on their Echo device or phone or to leave them a message. They must be in your phone's Contacts and be Alexa/Echo device users to be called. Here are the details:

1. Download the latest Alexa App for your iOS or Android phone from your app store.

2. Select the ***Conversations icon*** from the mobile app's home page (the middle icon of the three at the bottom of the screen). Follow the prompts to sign up for **Calling & Messaging** and verify your mobile number.

3. Import your contacts. The names of other signed-up Alexa/Echo device users will appear, so encourage friends and family who use Alexa to sign up.

4. Edit and add contacts in your phone's local address, as normal.

5. Open the Alexa app, and ask Alexa to call one of the signed-up contacts.

6. You can also call directly from the Alexa app on your phone. Choose the ***Conversations icon*** and tap a contact. Tap the ***phone icon*** for audio-only calls. Tap the ***camera icon*** for video calls.

7. You can call anyone from your Echo device if they have the Alexa app on their phone, whether they have an Echo or not. The call will go to their phone.

8. When you make a call, your Echo Show camera will deliver video to your recipient. Turn off the camera by pressing the Video icon that will appear on the touchscreen, or say, ***"Alexa, turn off video."***

9. When receiving a call, Alexa will tell you who is calling. The contact info will display on Echo Show and the light bar will

be green say, "*Alexa answer*" or tap the **Answer button**, or say, "*Ignore the call*". Say "*Alexa, hang up*" or tap the Show screen and the end-call button when you've completed the call.

10. Messaging is like leaving a voicemail or sending a text. To send a verbal message, say a contacts name. Alexa on Echo Show will guide you through the process.

11. To send a voice message from the mobile app, tap the *Conversations icon*, tap *New Conversation* and the contact you want to message. The prompts will walk you through the process. To type a message, at this point tap the *Keyboard icon*, type the message and select *Send*.

12. When you receive a message, Echo Show's light bar will be yellow. Say, "*Alexa, play my messages*" to hear them. If more than one mobile number is connected with the Alexa account, say, "*Alexa, play messages for Tom*," for example, to hear only your messages.

13. Reply to messages on the mobile app as you would reply to a text. For a voice reply, press the microphone icon on the Echo Show screen, and speak. Release it to send the message, or swipe left to cancel it and start again.

14. Contact Amazon customer service at 1.877.375.9365 with questions or to cancel Alexa Calling & Messaging.

A few tries with messaging will boost your confidence in using the technology. Once you're familiar with it, hands-free Calling on Alexa is easy and convenient.

Additional Help: If you want a refresher with visuals, go to **www. lyntons.com/ACandM**. Instructional videos for this and other topics can be found by going to **www.lyntons.com/Avideo**. In the Alexa app, view all Calling & Messaging topics at *Help & Feedback > Alexa > Alexa Calling and Messaging.*

Drop In: The Drop In tab and all the setup information needed is found in *About Amazon Alexa > Make Alexa-to-Alexa Calls and Messages*. Here's an overview of Drop In and the information/ links found in that section of the *Settings > Alexa User Guide*. The Drop In feature allows you to listen in on other Echo devices in your home, such as when using one as a baby or child monitor, and communicate directly with other Alexa/Echo users that have enabled Drop In without making a call

- *Drop In with same-house Echo devices:* The basic approach to using the Drop In feature in your home is to enable Drop In on the Alexa mobile app for each device. Remember that each Echo device will have its own name such as Jenna's Echo Show or Tom's Echo Dot. Then, using the app for Jenna's Echo Show, grant Tom's Echo Drop In permission and vice-versa. Once done, they can drop in on one another by saying *"Alexa drop in on Tom's Echo Dot,"* and end the drop in with, *"Alexa hang up."* Drop in can be controlled from the mobile app too.

- **Drop In with friends and family:** The approach is about the same. You use the Alexa mobile app and the Conversations icon at the bottom to select *Contacts* from your list and grant them Drop In permission. Both parties must enable Drop In and grant the other permission.

Privacy concerns are obvious. There are three levels of Permission:

- **On** - All contacts you have granted permission to can drop in anytime on your device

- **Only my household** - Only devices that are registered on your Alexa account can drop in

- **Off** - Drop in can be turned off on any device

Step-by-step instructions are buried in Settings at: *Help & Feedback > Alexa User Guide > About Calling & Messaging > Drop In*. There, you will find several sub-pages that will guide you through Use/Permissions/Remove Contacts and more.

Music, Video and Book

We haven't completely exhausted this topic. There are a few more things worth covering:

- **Play Music on Multiple Echo Devices:** This is a Smart Home feature that is easy to set up in six quick steps outlined in this section on the app: *Help & Feedback > Alexa User Guide > Music, Video & Books > Play Music on Multiple Echo Devices*. Form and Name the group as shown, and it will appear in the **Smart Home** page of your Alexa app under **Groups**. Then, request the music you want to hear and control it with voice, the app or your Echo Show the same way you would on one device. The one downside is that external Bluetooth speakers and other services like Audible and Flash Briefing don't yet work with this feature.

- **Set Up Alexa Connected Speaker Skills:** In this section, step-by-step directions are given to set up a Sonos or other external speaker to play your entire range of music. Find and enable the speaker's Skill in the Skill tab, sign in and link accounts, follow the onscreen prompts including logging into your Amazon account. Once that's set up, go to **Smart Home > Devices > Discover**. The two will sync, and you'll be playing music on the external speaker. Use the suggested requests given on the speaker's Skills page. **Tip:** If you haven't bought an external speaker yet, find the Skills page for those you're considering or search Speakers on the Skills tab. Read ratings and reviews about how the speaker works with Alexa. They'll provide insight that will produce a better purchasing decision.

- **Quick Fixes for Alexa Video Skills:** While we covered these in the troubleshooting section of the **Video Chapter**, it's worth keeping this part of Help & Feedback in mind in case you have problems that require deeper digging to solve.

Smart Home

There's lots of step-by-step guidance in this section of the Help & Feedback section to support what we discussed in **Chapter 14**. Let's look at a couple:

- **Use Smart Home Cameras with Alexa:** Turn Echo Show into a surveillance monitor. The key is to select a smart home camera supported on Alexa. Search the Skills tab for the camera you have. Optionally, search "camera" and see what cameras have Alexa Skills. When browsing possibilities, read the ratings and reviews for the Skill. Other users make very clear which Skills and supported equipment work/work well with Alexa and which don't. If you've tried setting up a camera without success, see **Having Trouble?** at the bottom of that page. There's excellent help there.

- **Remove a Smart Home Device:** If you want to remove a smart device from Alexa for any reason - it's not working and it's causing interference with other devices are common reasons - these four easy steps will get it done. You might also want to remove/forget the device if it needs to be reset or if you're having trouble with the initial connection

- **Supported Colors and Shades of White for Alexa Smart Light Control:** Smart lights are discussed in **Chapter 14**, but this list gives you all your color options when selecting colors and shades for supported smart bulbs.

Shopping

Alexa is a handy shopping tool, just what you'd expect from Amazon.

- **About Placing Orders on Amazon:** This topic is about setting up an Amazon Prime account, something we've covered and recommended, and the purchasing Prime-eligible items and Amazon's Choice items (highly rated, well-priced products, according to Amazon). If you don't have Prime, you can use Alexa to add items to your shopping cart on the website and to track order status. Finally of note, Primenow is Amazon's courier service for fast delivery of products and restaurant carryout. See **Primenow.amazon.com** for details.

- **Manage Voice Purchasing Options:** We're being a bit redundant here since this was covered in the Accounts Settings, but it's a significant feature of Alexa and Echo Show. If you have a Prime account, you can set up hands-free voice purchases, a feature we enjoy. You have to enable Voice Purchasing in *Settings > Accounts*. There, you can also add a 4-digit code that will be required before a voice sale will go through. We recommend the code to prevent accidental and unauthorized purchases.

- **Order an Alexa Device with our Voice:** Just one of your voice purchasing options, you can buy up to 12 Echo devices and up to 24 Echo Dots. Go for it! The holidays, birthdays, Father's Day, Mother's Day, Just Because... great gift ideas! The Echo Show purchase limit isn't currently listed, but if you say, "*Alexa, order an Echo Show*," your buying options appear on the Show screen with 1-click as an option for those that have set it up.

- **Track Open Orders with Alexa:** Very handy and as easy as asking, "*Alexa, where is my stuff?*" You can also turn on Notifications in *Settings > Notifications > Shopping Notifications* to read and/or hear notifications about when an Amazon order is out for delivery or has been left at your door.

- **Reorder from Amazon Restaurants with Alexa:** If you have a Prime membership, you can order meals from restaurants in your delivery area and then reorder the same thing with Alexa. Your default payment method will be used, and the meal will be delivered to your default address. The Amazon Restaurant Skill must be enabled. Currently it's hovering at 2.5 Stars out of 5, so you might want to review the ratings when you're reading this and read recent reviews to see if the service has improved. Find participating restaurants in your area at **Primenow.Amazon.com/restaurants**.

- **Cancel your Order:** If you have buyer's regret in the few minutes after placing an order, say, "*Alexa, cancel my order.*" If it was done in time, Alexa confirms that the order was cancelled. The rest of this section is about cancelling orders on the Amazon website if it's too late for Alexa to do it.

- **Alexa and Alexa Device FAQs:** Can't find answers anywhere else? Try here. Since the Help & Feedback section is so large that navigation can be frustrating, we'll give you the path to the FAQs: **Help & Feedback > Alexa > Shopping > Alexa and Alexa Device FAQs**. That's also an odd spot for it, in our opinion.

Alexa Quick Fixes

These topics have been covered "here and there" in this guide, but it is nice to have them all in one place. Here is how to find the section in the Alexa app and what topics are available: Go to **Help & Feedback > Alexa > Alexa Quick Fixes.**

- Alexa App doesn't work
- Alexa doesn't discover Your Smart Home device
- Quick fixes for using Alexa with Smart Home cameras
- Alexa doesn't understand you
- Bluetooth issues with Alexa devices
- Multi-room music quick fixes
- Streaming issues on Alexa devices
- Quick fixes for Alexa Skills

The Echo Show User Guide

Much of what is in this section on the app is redundant to the Alexa User Guide or has been covered along the way in this guide, but there are a few pertinent and new topics.

Echo Show Accessibility

There are three features that anyone with vision issues will benefit from knowing about. They are all managed on the Echo Show screen at **Settings > Accessibility**:

- **VoiceView Screen Reader:** This feature helps you find your way around the screen, so you can tap the function you want, by telling you what your fingers are touching. There's a walk-through, multi-lesson tutorial on Echo Show when you turn on VoiceView, and it is well worth your time. When VoiceView Reader is on:

1. Alexa reads what you're touching, and if it's the function you want, you can tap the screen anywhere two times to select do the function.

2. You can navigate To-do and Shopping Lists by hearing what you're touching and swiping the screen to move to the next item.

3. You can use the onscreen keypad and Alexa to add items to your list. As you drag your finger over the keypad, Alexa tells you what letter you're touching. When you are on the letter you want, lift your finger. It will be typed, and Alexa will confirm what it was.

4. The VoiceView tutorial can be returned to at any time. It's at the bottom of the VoiceView page.

5. There are specs you can adjust in the VoiceView. To scroll through the options for each, swipe left to go up one item; swipe right to go down one item.

- **Reading Speed:** Select how fast Alexa reads what you're touching. The default is 1x or Normal. Slowest is .66x, and fastest is 4x. We think most users will be comfortable with a speed above 1x but slower than 3x.

- **Speech Volume:** Your default option is to have things read at the level at which the device volume is set. We suggest using a slightly lower volume for two reasons. First, since you'll be using the touchscreen, you will be very close to it. Secondly, someone talking loudly, especially if at a higher-than-normal speed, can be irritating.

- **Sounds Volume:** Sometimes we're not conscious of the fact that devices give us little pings and chirps to affirm an action we took was completed. VoiceView uses a range of sounds as signals, since many users are visually impaired. Your options range from sounds Off to Match Device Volume, with 25% increments in between. If you have a hearing deficit, you'll want Match Volume. If not, something quieter might be appreciated.

- **Key Echo:** When typing on the onscreen keypad, you can hear key clicks when typing words, characters, both or neither.

- **Punctuation Level:** This option controls what punctuation marks Alexa reads to help you get the meaning of the content. These are helpful because Alexa's voice doesn't rise or fall as a human voice does to enhance meaning.

- **Screen Magnifier:** Turn this feature on to magnify what's on the Echo Show screen.

  1. Tap the screen three times, and it will be magnified.

  2. Place two fingers on the screen and move them apart to increase magnification.

  3. To turn off screen magnifier, hold the microphone (far left) button down until given an alert. Then, put two fingers on the screen slightly apart. Alexa will remind you that your action will turn off the feature. Keep your fingers in place until the screen returns to standard magnification.

- **Closed Captions:** Turn this feature on to enable Closed Captioning for video and movie trailers that support CC. Your Closed Caption settings options are found at ***Help & Feedback > Echo Show > Echo Show Accessibility > Used Closed Captions*** on Echo Show.

- **Color Inversion:** This feature inverts the color on the Echo Show screen. Black text on a white screen becomes white text on a black screen, as an example. The higher contrast against the light background improves readability for some users. However, we recommend turning this off while watching videos.

Color Correction: This feature will improve the experience for users with:

- Deuteranomaly - red/green
- Protanomaly - red/green
- Tritanomaly - blue/yellow

Echo Show Photos

You can take pictures with Echo Show and view all your photos on the device too.

Photo Booth: Take fun, hands-free pictures with Echo Show. Say, *"Alexa, take a photo,"* and Photo Booth will appear. Alexa will ask you to pick a camera, and you can select one of three options:

- Single-shot
- Sticker Mode using augmented reality - Slide left to see your Sticker Mode frames, stop on the one you want, and the countdown will start.
- Four-shot photo-booth style pictures

The photos are sent to Amazon Drive unless you have a Prime account with its unlimited photo storage. You can also slide all the way left when Alexa asks you to pick a camera. Your Photo Booth album will appear and play as a slideshow.

Slideshows: You can view a slideshow of your photos on Echo Show from two sources:

- **Amazon Drive:** Everyone with an Amazon account has a free membership to Amazon Drive, storage in the cloud. This includes 5GB of free space for photos, files, video, music and more. An upgrade to 100GB costs $11.99/year. A plan with 1TB of storage costs $59.99/year.
- **Amazon Prime:** If you have a Prime membership, Prime Photos offers unlimited photo storage in the Amazon cloud.

Once you have photos stored on Amazon, you can ask Alexa to see them on Echo Show with phrases that tap into how you've named, grouped and added your photos. Some examples are: *"Alexa..."*

- *"Show my photos"*
- *"Show today's photos"*
- *"Show my puppies album"*
- *"Show my photos of Taiwan"*
- *"Show my photos from January"*

A more complete list of suggestions of what to say is found at ***Help & Feedback > Echo Show > Echo Show Photos > View Photos on Echo Show***.

On the Echo Show, choose **S***ettings > **Display > Photo Slideshow*** to manage two settings:

- **Slideshow Display:** Smart Cropping/No Cropping
- **Slideshow Speed:** Slow (10 seconds), Medium (6) or Fast (2)

Contact Us

If you have stubborn problems with the Alexa app or Echo Show, Amazon Customer Service is helpful and timely. Email and phone give you options for your preferred way to communicate.

E-mail Customer Service: Select a device you have questions about, select a category closest and specific issue, and tell Amazon all about it.

Be Called by Customer Service: Use the same form to choose a device, category and issue, and then leave your phone number before selecting the best time to be called.

Send Feedback: Send Amazon your thoughts on Alexa and Echo Show. Be sure to select the box if you want Amazon to follow-up by contacting you.

A Final Quick Reminder About Updates

As we mentioned at the start of this book, the Amazon Echo Show and indeed the whole Echo family of devices are still in their infancy. The landscape is changing all the time with new services, apps and media suppliers appearing daily. Staying on top of new developments is our job and if you sign up to our free newsletter we will keep you abreast of news, tips and tricks for all your streaming media equipment.

If you want to take advantage of this, sign up for the updates here **www.lyntons.com/updates**

 Don't worry; we hate spam as much as you do so we will never share your details with anyone.

Made in the USA
Lexington, KY
21 June 2018